Praise for *Iran Awakening*:

'The riveting story of an amazing and very brave woman living through some quite turbulent times. And she emerges with head unbowed' Archbishop Desmond Tutu

'One of the staunchest advocates for human rights in her country and beyond, Ms Ebadi, herself a devout Muslim, represents hope for many in Muslim societies that Islam and democracy are indeed compatible' Azar Nafisi, author of *Reading Lolita in Tehran*

'A complex and moving portrait of a life lived in truth, as Vaclav Havel would put it'
The New York Times Book Review

'With Islam as her starting point, Ebadi campaigns for peaceful solutions to social problems, and promotes new thinking on Islamic terms. She has displayed great personal courage'
The Times of India

'An incredible memoir . . . beautifully written. This is a book infused with humanity and astounding hope'
The Works

Iran Awakening

FROM PRISON TO PEACE PRIZE:
ONE WOMAN'S STRUGGLE AT THE
CROSSROADS OF HISTORY

SHIRIN EBADI

Winner of the Nobel Peace Prize

WITH AZADEH MOAVENI

RIDER

LONDON · SYDNEY · AUCKLAND · JOHANNESBURG

5 7 9 10 8 6

Copyright © 2006 by Shirin Ebadi
Map copyright © 1997 by Anita Karl and Jim Kemp

First published by Random House,
Random House, Inc., New York in 2006.
This edition published in 2006 by Rider,
an imprint of Ebury Publishing, Random House,
20 Vauxhall Bridge Road, London SW1V 2SA
www.randomhouse.co.uk

Random House Australia (Pty) Limited
20 Alfred Street, Milsons Point, Sydney,
New South Wales 2061, Australia

Random House New Zealand Limited
18 Poland Road, Glenfield,
Auckland 10, New Zealand

Random House South Africa (Pty) Limited
Isle of Houghton, Corner of Boundary Road & Carse O'Gowrie,
Houghton 2198, South Africa

Random House Publishers India Private Limited
301 World Trade Tower, Hotel Intercontinental Grand Complex,
Barakhamba Lane, New Delhi 110 001, India

The Random House Group Limited Reg. No. 954009

Printed by Cox & Wyman Ltd, Reading, Berkshire

A CIP catalogue record for this book is available from the British Library

ISBN 9781846040146

In memory

of my mother and my older sister, Mina,

both of whom passed away

during the writing of this book.

Sadness to me is the happiest time,
When a shining city rises from the ruins of my drunken mind.
Those times when I'm silent and still as the earth,
The thunder of my roar is heard across the universe.

—MOWLANA JALALEDDIN RUMI

✡

I swear by the declining day, that perdition shall be the lot of man. Except for those who have faith and do good works and exhort each other to justice and fortitude.

—THE HOLY KORAN 103:3

Contents

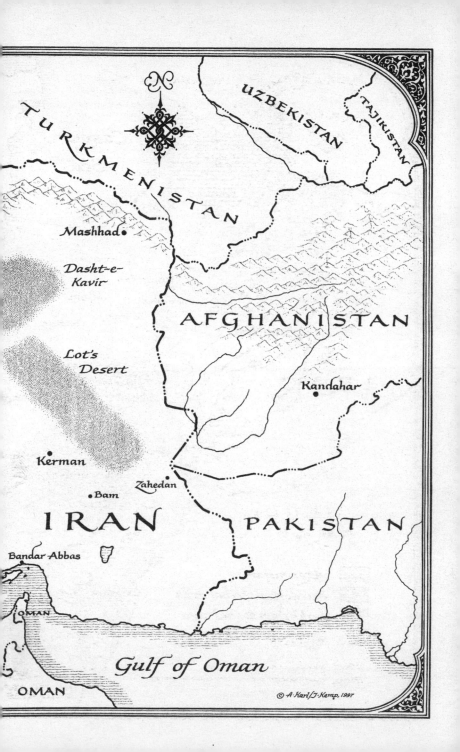

Prologue

IN THE FALL OF 2000, NEARLY A DECADE AFTER I BEGAN my legal practice defending victims of violence in the courts of Iran, I faced the ten most harrowing days of my entire career. The work I typically handled— battered children, women hostage to abusive marriages, political prisoners—brought me into daily contact with human cruelty, but the case at hand involved menace of a different order. The government had recently admitted partial complicity in the premeditated spate of killings in the late nineties that took the lives of dozens of intellectuals. Some were strangled while out running errands, others hacked to death in their homes. I represented the family of two of the victims, and anxiously awaited seeing the files of the judiciary's investigation.

The presiding judge had granted the victims' lawyers only ten days to read the entire dossier. Those brief days would be our only access to the investigation's findings, our only chance to dig up evidence to build our case. The disarray of the investigation, the attempts to cover up the state's hand, and the mysterious prison suicide of a lead suspect compounded our difficulty in piecing together an account of what had truly transpired, from the fatwas ordering the killings to their execution. The stakes could not be higher. It was the first time in the history of the Islamic Republic that the state had acknowledged that it had murdered its critics, and the first time a trial would be convened to hold the perpetrators accountable. The government itself had admitted that a rogue squad within the Ministry of Intelligence was responsible for the killings, but the case had not yet gone to trial. When the time finally rolled around, we arrived at the courthouse, tense with determination.

After surveying the sheer physical volume of the files, stacks as tall as our heads, we realized that we would have to read them concurrently and, therefore, except for one of us, out of order. In deference, the other lawyers of the victims' families allowed me to start at the beginning, so each page I hurriedly turned, my eyes were the first to see.

The sun shone through the dirty windowpane, its rays moving across the room too quickly as we hunched shoulder to shoulder over the small table, silent save for the rustle of papers and the occasional thump of my wooden chair's stump leg. The significant passages in the files, the transcripts of the interrogations of the accused killers, were scattered throughout, buried in pages of bureaucratic filler. The material was dark with descriptions of the brutal murders, passages where a killer, with seeming relish, told of crying out "*Ya Zahra,*" in dark homage to the Prophet Mohammed's daughter, with each stab. In the room next door, the defendants' lawyers sat reading other parts of the dossier, and it was impossible not to feel their presence radiating through the wall, these men who were defending those who had murdered in the name of God. Most of them were low-ranking functionaries of the Ministry of Intelligence, henchmen who had executed the death lists at the behest of more senior officials.

At around noon, our energy flagged, and one of the lawyers called to the young soldier in the hall to bring us some tea. The moment the tea tray arrived, we bent our heads down again. I had reached a page more detailed, and more narrative, than any previous section, and I slowed down to focus. It was the transcript of a conversation between a government minister and a member of the death squad. When my eyes first fell on the sentence that would haunt me for years to come, I thought I had misread. I blinked once, but it stared back at me from the page: "The next person to be killed is Shirin Ebadi." Me.

My throat went dry. I read the line over and over again, the printed words blurring before me. The only other woman in the room, Parastou Forouhar, whose parents had been the first to be killed, stabbed and viciously mutilated in their Tehran home in the middle of the night, sat next to me. I pressed her arm and nodded toward the page. She bent her veiled head close and scanned from the top. "Did you read it? Did you read it?" she kept whispering. We read on together, read of my would-be assassin going to the minister of intelligence, requesting permission to execute my killing. Not during the fasting month of Ramadan, the minister had replied, but anytime thereafter. But they don't fast anyway, the mercenary had argued; these people have divorced God. It was through this belief—that the intellectuals, that I, had abandoned God—that they justified the killings as religious duty. In the grisly terminology of those who interpret Islam violently, our blood was considered halal, its spilling permitted by God.

At that moment, the door creaked open. More tea, flavorless cups that cluttered the table but kept us alert. I distracted myself by rearranging the papers in front of me, my mind reeling from what I had read. I wasn't scared, really, nor was I angry. I remember mostly an overwhelming feeling of disbelief. Why do they hate me so much? I wondered. What have I done to elicit hate of this order? How have I created such enemies, so eager to spill my blood that they cannot wait for Ramadan to end?

We didn't stop to talk about it then; there was no time for gasps, or sympathetic murmurings of "How awful that you were next on the list." We couldn't waste any of our limited, precious time with the files. I sipped my tea and went on, though my fingers felt paralyzed and I turned the pages with difficulty. At around two o'clock we finished, and it was only then that I told the other lawyers, as we passed through the courtyard outside. They shook their heads, murmured, *Alhamdolellah*, thanks to God; unlike the victims whose families we were defending, I had evaded death.

I stepped into the welcoming cacophony of Tehran traffic, the wide streets and low-slung buildings overrun that time of day by wheezing old cars. I took a taxi home, lulled by the vibration of the dusty Paykan beneath me until we reached my house. I ran inside, peeled off my clothes, and stayed under the shower for an hour, letting the cool water cascade over me, rinsing off the filth of those files, lodged in my mind, under my fingernails. Only after dinner, after my daughters went to bed, did I tell my husband. *So, something interesting happened to me at work today*, I began.

Iran Awakening

CHAPTER ONE

A Tehran Girlhood

MY INDULGENT GRANDMOTHER, WHO NEVER SPOKE TO us children in anything but honeyed tones of endearment, snapped at us for the first time on August 19, 1953. We were playing in the corner of the shadowed, lantern-lit living room when she turned on us with a stern expression and scolded us quiet. It was the year before I started grade school, and my family was spending the summer at my father's spacious country home on the outskirts of Hamedan, a province in central western Iran where both of my parents were raised. My grandmother also owned property nearby, and the grandchildren gathered there each summer, playing hide-and-seek in the fruit orchards and returning by sunset to gather around the radio with the adults. I vividly recall that evening: we returned home with sticky fingers and berry-stained clothes to find the adults in a terrible mood, for once unmoved by our disarray. They sat huddled around the radio, closer than usual, with rapt expressions, the copper bowls of dates and pistachios before them untouched. A trembling voice announced on the battery-operated radio that after four days of turmoil in Tehran, Prime Minister Mohammad

Mossadegh had been toppled in a coup d'état. To us children, this news meant nothing. We giggled at the downcast eyes and somber faces of the adults and scampered away from the still, funereal living room.

The supporters of the shah who seized the national radio network announced that with the fall of Mossadegh the Iranian people had triumphed. Few outside those paid to participate in the coup d'état actually shared this sentiment. For secular and religious Iranians, working class and wealthy alike, Mossadegh was far more than a popular statesman. To them, he was a beloved nationalist hero, a figure worthy of their zealous veneration, a leader fit to guide their great civilization, with its more than twenty-five hundred years of recorded history. Two years prior, in 1951, the prime minister had nationalized Iran's oil industry, until then effectively controlled by Western oil consortiums, which extracted and exported vast stores of Iranian oil under agreements that allotted Iran only a slim share of the profits. This bold move, which upset the West's calculations in the oil-rich Middle East, earned Mossadegh the eternal adoration of Iranians, who viewed him as the father figure of Iranian independence, much as Mahatma Gandhi was revered in India for freeing his nation from the British Empire. Democratically elected to power by overwhelming consensus in 1951, Mossadegh extended his popularity beyond the appeal of his nationalism. His open demands for freedom of the press, his penchant for conducting diplomacy from his bed, his Swiss education, and his Iranian savvy combined to enchant people, who saw in him a brilliant, cunning leader who embodied not just their aspirations but their intricate conception of self—like them, he was composed of seeming contradictions, aristocratic roots and populist ambitions, secular sensibilities that never precluded alliances with powerful clerics.

The Iranian constitution of 1906, which established the modern constitutional monarchy, vested only symbolic power in the hands of the monarchy. Under the reign of Reza Shah, from 1926 to 1941, a wise dictator and nation builder who assumed total authority with a measure of popular support, the monarchy ran the country. But in 1941, after British and Russian forces occupied Iran during World War II, Reza Shah was forced to abdicate the throne in favor of his son, Mohammad Reza Pahlavi. The young shah presided over a period of relative political openness marked by a freer press, and the balance of power shifted back toward elected government, with the parliament and its appointed prime minister taking control of the country's affairs as the constitution had intended. During Prime Minister Mossadegh's brief era, the shah exerted nominal influence, and until the coup d'état of 1953, it could be said that the Iranian people were effectively governed by their elected representatives.

In 1951, next to the prime minister, the unloved thirty-two-year-old shah, heir to a newly minted, unpopular dynasty conceived of by a Persian Cossack army officer, appeared a green inferiority of little promise. The shah observed Mossadegh's rise with anxiety. In the expansive popular support for the prime minister, he confronted his own vulnerability as an unpopular monarch backed only by his generals, the United States, and Britain. The two Western powers were incensed by Mossadegh's nationalization of Iranian oil, but they bided their time before launching a response. In 1953, they concluded that circumstances were auspicious for his overthrow. Kermit Roosevelt, a grandson of Teddy Roosevelt, arrived in Tehran to reassure the skittish shah and direct the coup d'état. With nearly a million dollars at his disposal, he paid crowds in poor south Tehran to march in protest and bribed newspaper editors to run spurious headlines of swelling anti-Mossadegh discontent. In a neat four days, the ailing, adored prime minister was hiding in a cellar and the venal young shah was restored to power, famously thanking Kermit Roosevelt: "I owe my throne to God, my people, my army, and to you." It was a profoundly humiliating moment for Iranians, who watched the United States intervene in their politics as if their country were some annexed backwater, its leader to be installed or deposed at the whim of an American president and his CIA advisers.

The shah ordered a military trial for Mossadegh, and newspapers ran front-page photos of the fallen prime minister entering the crowded courtroom, his gaunt frame and aquiline features more striking than ever. The judge handed down a death sentence but said he would reduce it to three years in prison, in tribute to the shah's superior mercy. For those three years, Mossadegh languished in a central Tehran prison; afterward, he retired to his village of Ahmadabad, to spend his retirement responding to letters from his devastated and still loyal supporters. In later years, his replies, penned in his subtle, lucid handwriting, appeared framed in the offices of Iran's leading opposition figures, those who would a quarter century later thrust the shah from power in the 1979 revolution.

*T*welve years before the coup that interrupted both Iranian history and their lives, my parents met and married in the fashion typical for Iranians of their generation: through the traditional courtship ritual known as *khastegari*. On a bright spring afternoon in 1945, with the cool mountain breeze blowing across the ancient city of Hamedan, my father presented himself at my mother's family home to ask for her hand in marriage. They were distant relatives, and had met several months earlier at the home of a second cousin. The family received him in the formal sitting room reserved for company, and my mother served tea and *shirini* (the word means "sweets," and shares an origin with my name), peeking at my father's handsome profile while carefully pouring the cardamom-laced tea in the graceful manner long practiced for precisely this occasion. He fell deeply in love with her from the start, and to this day I have yet to see a man adore a woman more devotedly than he did my mother. Throughout their long lives, he addressed her reverentially as Minu *khanum*, adding the formal Persian word for "lady" after her name, as though he feared familiarity would diminish his regard. She called him Mohammad-Ali Khan.

When my mother was growing up, she dreamed of attending medical school and becoming a doctor. But before the day of the *khastegari,* the family roundly dismissed this possibility, on grounds that my mother scarcely had control over. As she entered adolescence, it escaped no one's notice that she was becoming a rather spectacular beauty. Had she been born a generation earlier, when it was unheard of for women to attend college, her luminous, fair skin and slender figure might have conferred some advantage in the only realm in which she could compete, the marriage bazaar. But for a young woman born in the late 1920s, a time when patriarchy was slowly loosening its grip on Iranian society and a few women were being admitted into universities, her good looks were a liability to any ambition greater than marriage.

She did not wear the veil, for her family was not so traditional as to insist that its girls cover their hair. But she did witness the banning of the *hejab,* as part of the modernization campaign launched by Reza Shah, who crowned himself king of Iran in 1926. Turning an expansive country of villages and peasants overnight into a central-

My mother.

ized nation with railroads and a legal code was a complex task. Reza Shah believed it would be impossible without the participation of the country's women, and he set about emancipating them by banning the veil, the symbol of tradition's yoke. Reza Shah was the first, but not the last, Iranian ruler to act out a political agenda—secular modernization, shrinking the clergy's influence—on the frontier of women's bodies.

Circumstance and era conspired to keep my mother from a university education, but at least she ended up marrying a man as unpatriarchal as could be imagined, for his time. My father was serene by temperament, controlled his anger without fail, and could never be provoked into raising his voice. When upset or irritated, he paced the house with his hands behind him or methodically rolled a cigar, extracting tobacco from a silver case carefully, using the time to still his mind and raising his head only when he was fully composed.

He was born into a wealthy family, to a landowning father who served as a colonel in the military, in the late days of the Qajar dynasty, the monarchy that preceded Reza Shah's. My grandfather had married a Qajar princess whom he loved dearly, but who could not bear him children. After painful years of trying, he finally relented to the insistence of his brothers and, with his wife's approval, acquired a second wife, Shahrbanu, who gave birth to my father and uncle. My grandfather passed away when my father was seven, leaving Shahrbanu alone with two children. The relatives fought over his will and eventually stripped the widowed Shahrbanu of much of his property and wealth. Indignant, she decided to fight back. She traveled to Qom, Iran's holiest city and home to the country's seminaries, hoping to find clerics who would help her secure custody of her children and the holdings that remained. With their assistance, she managed to keep her two sons, as well as assets enough to meet the family's basic needs. In those days, women's consciousness of their rights was limited to their intuitive sense of right and wrong; they would not have conceived of petitioning a legal system for redress, and instead appealed to influential men in society—often clerics, seen as a resource for battling injustices large and small—to advocate on their behalf.

I was born on June 21, 1947, the summer before we left Hamedan for Tehran. My childhood memories revolve around our home in the capital, on what was then called Shah Street (renamed, like most of the city's streets, after the Islamic Revolution). The house was quite large, two stories tall and full of rooms, a veritable playground for my siblings and me. In the manner of old Iranian homes, it was built around a central courtyard garden full of roses and white lilies. There was a pool in the middle where a few silvery fish swam, and on summer evenings our beds were carried outside, so that we could fall asleep under the stars, the air perfumed with flowers and the night's silence filled with the chirping of crickets. My mother kept the house spotless—clutter of any sort irritated her—and in this she was assisted by our household staff. Many of my father's farmworkers from Hamedan had applied to serve at our house in Tehran. She entrusted each servant with a task; one did the shopping, another cooked, the third cleaned, and the fourth served tea and meals to guests.

My mother seemed to genuinely love my father, though their marriage had been essentially arranged, and had kept her from attending college. She would wait impatiently for his deep, booming voice to resound through the courtyard at the day's end. But after her marriage, she developed an extraordinarily anxious temperament. If we came home five minutes late, we would find her in the alley outside our house, frantic with fear that we had been kidnapped or run over by a car. The nervousness manifested itself in her physical health as well, and she was often ill, in and out of the care of doctors unable to fully treat or diagnose the source of her constant agitation. There was no obvious reason for it. By almost any account, she was a perfectly fortunate woman—cared for by an ideal, loving husband, mother to obedient, healthy children, in relatively good social and financial standing. It would have been enough to make most Iranian women of her day content. But I can't recall a single day when my mother seemed truly happy.

As I grew older, my mother still groomed herself immaculately, still smiled quietly as she sat knitting in the shadiest corner of our spotless house, but the anxieties still raged inside her, and her body revolted with one illness after another. She was perpetually sick, and her attention to her failing health only fed her nervousness. For a while she came down with asthma, and she paced the house, complaining of feeling suffocated. When I was fourteen, my older sister married and moved back to Hamedan, leaving me the eldest child at home. My mother's poor health was the backdrop of our lives, and I constantly feared her death. I would lie awake at night, staring at the ceiling through the gauze of mosquito netting, worrying about my brother and sisters. What would happen to them if our mother died? Each night, I entreated God to keep her alive until my little brother and sister grew up. In my young mind, I thought that if she died I would have to quit school and take on her duties at home.

One day that year I crept up to the attic, to make a quiet appeal to God. Please, please keep my mother alive, I prayed, so I can stay in school. Suddenly, an indescribable feeling overtook me, starting in my stomach and spreading to my fingertips. In that stirring, I felt as though God was answering me. My sadness evaporated, and a strange euphoria shot through my heart. Since that moment, my faith in God has been unshakable. Before that day I had only said my prayers by rote, because I had been taught to say them, just as I had been taught to wash my face before bed. But after that moment in the attic, I began to recite them with true belief. It is hard to describe the awakening of spirituality, just as it is difficult to explain to someone who has never fallen in love the emotional contours of that experience. My attic revelation reminds me of a line from a Persian poem, "Oh you, the stricken one / Love comes to you, it is not learned."

Me as a junior in high school.

Throughout most of my childhood years—as is the way with children, whose family is the only world they know—I never observed that our household was special. It didn't strike me as exceptional that my parents did not treat my brother differently from their daughters. It seemed perfectly natural, and I assumed everyone else's families were the same way. They most certainly were not. In most Iranian households, male children enjoyed an exalted status, spoiled and cosseted by a coterie of aunts and female relatives. They often felt themselves the center of the family's orbit. Their rebellion was overlooked or praised, and their taste in food became the chief concern of the kitchen. As children grew older, the boys' privileges—from running about the neighborhood to consorting with a range of friends—expanded, while the girls' contracted, to ensure that they remain *najeeb*, honorable and well-bred. In Iranian culture, it was considered natural for fathers to love their sons more; the sons were the repository for the family's future ambitions; affection for a son was an investment.

In our house, my parents meted out attention, affection, and discipline equally. I never felt that my father cared about Jafar more because he was the only boy, or that Jafar was more special than I was. All of our comings and goings had to be punctual, and accounted for, until we reached high school. I was allowed to go to the movies or attend parties with my friends only after high school, and these same rules also applied to my brother.

At times, my father's evenhanded way of dealing with us children perplexed the household staff. The servants viewed my brother as their future boss, and they expected to see him exercise his influence over the opposite sex from a young age. Naturally, their own traditional upbringings had taught them that boys deserved special independence and freedom, grooming them for the authority they would assert as men. Since I was five years older than my brother, I typically won our fights. My parents never punished or scolded me; instead, they mediated gently, as though brokering a serious peace between adults. The house staff complained loudly, appalled by this breakdown in social order. "Why are you allowing a girl to hit Jafar Khan?" they would ask my father. He would merely smile, and reply, "They're children, they'll make up themselves."

It was not until I was much older that I realized how gender equality was impressed on me first and foremost at home, by example. It was only when I surveyed my own sense of place in the world from an adult perspective that I saw how my upbringing spared me from the low self-esteem and learned dependence that I observed in women reared in more traditional homes. My father's championing of my independence, from the play yard to my later decision to become a judge, instilled a confidence in me that I never felt consciously, but later came to regard as my most valued inheritance.

When I think back to those early years, most of my recollections drift between Hamedan and Tehran, and apart from my religious epiphany in the attic, none of them are fixed in significance or time, except the day Mossadegh was overthrown—the day Iran's first democratically elected leader was tossed out of the government in a coup organized by the CIA and its puppet. Though I can hardly recall what came before, and only loose fragments of what came later, and though at the time I had little sense of the day's fateful significance, I remember the faces of the adults, my grandmother's tone, and even the wooden gleam of the radio.

Only over a quarter century later, when the Islamic Revolution overthrew the shah and radicals took the American embassy hostage, did I see how the long arc of the coup had worked its away across our twentieth-century history. But in those early days, when I was still a child, I first perceived the impact of Mossadegh's overthrow at home. My father, a longtime supporter of the ousted prime minister, was forced out of his job. Before the coup, he had advanced to become deputy minister of agriculture. For years after it, he languished in lower posts, and he was never appointed at the senior level again. The legacy of my father's sidelining was that our house became an irredeemably politics-free zone. He initially became housebound, pacing the halls throughout the day, instead of just in the evening. He never explained to us children what had happened, why suddenly our father was home all day, pensive and quiet. When something terrible happens, it is most Iranians' first instinct to hide it from their children, who notice immediately that something has gone wrong and must then add the burden of ignorance to their disquiet. From those years on, I resolved to be different, and to speak openly with my own children about calamities.

The coup convinced many Iranians that politics was dirty, an intricate game of backroom deals and cloaked interests in which ordinary people were pawns; it fed the sense that we were not masters of our own destiny, as well as the tendency to believe that the ramifications of an event determined its origins. After that day, my father refused to discuss politics at home, so that his children would grow up untainted by an interest in processes they could not affect. Convinced that one destroyed career was enough for any family, he insisted we should attend excellent universities and serve the country as technocrats. As a result, my growing up was singular in another way: I was oblivious to politics, except for that night in 1953.

CHAPTER TWO

Discovering Justice

THE YEAR I ENTERED LAW SCHOOL, 1965, WAS A TURNING point for me. The intellectually charged campus of Tehran University was caught up in the increasingly heated politics of a wider Iran, changes that I—in the politics-free zone imposed by my father—was scarcely aware of. When I'd decided to attend law school, I'd never imagined that law students would be so absorbed in national politics. That year was my first introduction to university life altogether, for in Iran going to law school was the equivalent of an extended undergraduate degree in the field of law. In the late spring of 1965, when choosing my field of higher study, I had contemplated political science, occasionally envisioning myself as an ambassador. But in all honesty, I knew I stood a better chance at passing the *concours*, the stringent college entrance examination, for the faculty of law, which played to my academic strengths. In the Iranian justice system, a judge is not required to first practice law, and I set out in my studies intent on a judgeship. My class was filled with students who aimed to become legal scholars, experts, or, like me, judges. Though we spent hours in the library poring over texts of criminal law, trying to devise contemporary case studies, most of my classmates focused equally, if not more, on the politics brewing around them.

One clear afternoon, they shouted that the tuition was too high. They shouted for the university administration to be accountable. Basically, the crowd of students gathered at Tehran University shouted anything that would not immediately get them arrested. Standing among the assembled protesters, the women in their miniskirts and elaborate beehives, the young men in short sleeves with serious faces, I felt a crackle of energy pass through me. Protests attracted me like a magnet. What the students were chanting hardly mattered. Mostly they demonstrated against tuition fees, but even if they had protested the soaring price of tea, I probably would have turned up. Something about confrontation—perhaps the adrenaline, the spark of an idea, the fleeting sense of agency—appealed to me, and I attended protests regularly. Fortunately, because it was the late 1960s and students demonstrated nearly every other day, I never faced a shortage.

The demonstrations provoked the anxiety of the SAVAK, the shah's secret police, which actively combed the campus, as it combed the streets of most of Iran's cities, as it combed Iranian student groups in the United States and Europe, to root out dissidents whose political activities went beyond fashionably dropping in on demonstrations. For what Iranian young person—religious or secular, intellectual or socialite, serious or just curious—did not attend the occasional protest? It took the energies and resources of a massive police apparatus to ferret out who was truly organizing to undermine the shah's regime and who was just checking out what all the commotion was about. To evade the tentacles of the SAVAK, students pretended to protest tuition fees, though what they really wanted to chant was more like "Stop squandering our oil revenue on fleets of American fighter planes!" or "Come back from St. Moritz and deal with urban poverty, please!"

That day I scanned about for my girlfriends, my gaze moving past the arching trees and monotonous but sleek buildings of the expansive campus, one of the few decent universities in a country whose oil revenue should have afforded many more. Like most of my friends scattered among the crowd that day, I scarcely suspected that such protests were the beginning of an era. I never imagined that they would one day alter the course of our lives, send shock waves around the world, and produce the twentieth century's last great revolution. They were the background of our lives at the university, an afternoon shot of adrenaline before we walked over to the coffeehouse near the university where we sipped *café glace*, vanilla ice cream drowned in coffee, after class.

That day, however, unlike most, we skipped the coffeehouse, for one of my girlfriends had a clunky white Paykan parked on the street. Six of us piled into the car, and we began heading north toward Darband, where cafés and restaurants dotted the low swell of the Alborz, the mountains that rim the northernmost edge of the city. You might think that because we had just come from a protest, our conversation would at least border on the serious. Not really. We gossiped about classmates, films, the destination of our next road trip, the sort of thing young female college students talk about. In the university milieu of the time, it was fashionable to affect intellectual airs, and to skillfully dissect the shah's flaws in conversation, but to be truthful about it, we were not very much bothered about such questions.

As we crawled north, traffic hurtling past us in the other direction, the transformation of Tehran from a discrete capital surrounded by orchards to a sprawling urban metropolis was everywhere on display. Construction scaffolding adorned every other corner, trucks hauling bags of cement and planks of wood traversed the city like worker ants, movie billboards showcasing European film stars loomed above busy squares, and kiosks hawked magazines of bikini-clad American starlets. It was a different city already than the Tehran of my girlhood: more slums, more restaurants, more movie theaters, more provincial young men in dusty clothes and mud-caked boots en route to and from their varied labors.

Curious to see for ourselves the fabled elegance of Darband's French restaurants, we had saved our pocket money for three days in anticipation of a spectacular lunch. The spot we chose overlooked the trickling river that wound down through the foothills of the Alborz, its tastefully arranged tables set against the gleaming windows. A crisply dressed waiter handed us menus, and we scanned the exorbitant prices in alarm. There was no way we could afford anything more than a beverage, so to extricate ourselves, we decided to ask for the one thing we knew they would not serve: *kabob-koobideh,* a modest skewer of ground beef that had no place among the gratins and coq au vin that dominated the menu. The waiter shook his head, and we got up from the table, affecting looks of deep disappointment.

That day we learned to ignore accounts of Tehran's higher-end delights, the Greek restaurant where they broke plates, or the terrace cafés where glitteringly dressed couples listened to the Four Tops while sipping vodka tonics. We limited our outings to the more

With classmates in college. I'm in the middle.

moderate restaurants of Shemiran—a name that demarcates north Tehran both geographically and figuratively—where three of us could pool resources and split a bowl of ice cream.

We socialized, in mixed groups of men and women, along such wholesome lines. True, it was the era of the miniskirt, and around the university—indeed, all around the city—stylish young women bared their legs in homage to Twiggy, the fashion icon of the moment. But the mimicking of Western fashion amounted to little more than a trend. The students at Tehran University came from middle- or working-class backgrounds and didn't view their social lives as a realm for experimentation. We didn't wear veils—in fact, the three veiled women in our university class stood out—but neither did we date, in the Western sense of the word. We always gathered for coffees or weekend trips in mixed groups, and though men and women studied together in the library, in class women still occupied the front rows, and men the back.

With college friends. I'm in the middle.

To conservative clerics, the university was a den of corruption, a polluted place where men and women sinned under the pretext of coed learning. To traditionally minded households, overseen by fathers who preferred to keep their daughters out of school, enclosed in the courtyards of the home, mincing herbs for the evening's dinner, the advent of the miniskirt became a symbol of Western cultural invasion, the perfect excuse to invoke against the possibility of a university education.

As the 1960s drew to a close, the political atmosphere in the country steadily became more charged. In 1964, the year before I had started law school, the shah had expelled a little-known, scowling cleric, Ayatollah Ruhollah Khomeini, to Najaf, Iraq, because of his fiery sermons that cleverly attacked the government. But with the ayatollah in absentia, no ideology or leader had yet emerged for anti-shah sentiment to coalesce around. It made opposing the shah easy, for most people not immediately connected to the court elite had some form of grievance, and a critical stance did not immediately align you with a distinct opposing camp. To be anti-shah, in those days, did not mean you were pro—Ayatollah Khomeini. Often when I heard fragments of political conversations in the halls, it seemed to me students were becoming more and more anti-shah without knowing why, as though it were a badge of intellectual status, like reading Simone de Beauvoir.

One morning in French class, one of the fourth-year law students walked into the classroom late, dressed in black from head to toe. We all assumed one of his relatives had passed away, and inquired gently. "I'm in mourning for Mossadegh," he announced. We assumed he meant our classmate Hamid Mossadegh, a popular young poet we occasionally met for tea in the cafeteria. "So young! How horrible! Did he have cancer?" we gasped, going on woefully about how unfair it was to die young. "I mean *Dr.* Mossadegh," the black-clad young man interrupted. "Oh, he was quite old anyway, no matter!" we said, sighing in relief. He stared at us aghast, turned on his heels, and didn't speak to us for a week.

After the news filled the papers and I noticed my father's reaction at home, my impudence filled me with remorse. Former prime minister Mohammad Mossadegh was not simply a fallen statesman but one of our history's greatest leaders, who had presided over the first flush of democracy Iran had experienced in centuries. Even in his final years, before he fell seriously ill with cancer and died in a Tehran hospital, the reverberations of his truncated career could be felt around the country. Mossadegh's overthrow had set a permanent grudge with the West, particularly America, that grew only more rancorous with time. Although the old prime minister died of natural causes, he was mourned as a great hero-martyr, felled in an epic battle. The intensity of young Iranians' grief also reflected their growing alienation with the shah's regime, which grew less diffuse and more acute each day.

In March 1970, at the age of twenty-three, I became a judge. The Iranian legal system did not set a minimum age for the position. I, along with the other twenty or so women in my class, had spent the last two years of law school interning in the various branches of the Ministry of Justice. In many cases, once the district judges felt we had sufficiently mastered the legal code, they permitted us to preside over the courtroom. Upon graduating from law school, having fulfilled two years of internship experience, we were eligible to become judges.

At the swearing-in ceremony, attended by the minister of justice, high-ranking judges, and professors of the college of law, the top two students in the class had to carry an immense Koran to the podium. I was very short, and the other top student was extremely tall. As we hobbled across the stage the Koran swayed back and forth awkwardly, tilting to one side. "Lower your hands," I hissed at my fellow Koran bearer, struggling to keep balance. "Raise yours," he whispered back. Finally we managed to lug the heavy holy book to its destination, and I delivered my speech in a loud, crystal voice. I read the oath, the other students repeated after me, and we stepped down from the stage, toward what we believed with great faith would be a lifetime of serving justice.

The timing of my career's onset made it possible for me to join an institution of an unpopular government yet still not feel that I had to take sides. Most Iranians chafed under the excess and repression of the shah's rule, but this discontent did not translate into an all-out divide between people and regime, or a extension of mistrust to branches of government such as the judiciary. Though they quaked at the very notion of the SAVAK, people still trusted the legal system and sincerely believed that the laws protected their rights.

Me on the day I graduated from law school.
I was twenty-two.

Even I, who was slowly starting to pay attention to the political chatter around me, put on my skirt suit each morning and drove to a Ministry of Justice I felt proud to represent. The shah's regime prosecuted its political opponents in military courts, and kept those kangaroo trials out of the public justice system. In the military courts, dissidents faced the vague umbrella charges—sabotage, jeopardizing national security, and the like—that repressive regimes reserve for any activity they view as threatening. But the legal system most Iranians appealed to for anything from divorce to fraud operated in parallel, and as a consequence remained largely fair and uncorrupt in people's minds.

We did not usually keep the television on at the ministry, but on the day in 1971 when the shah displayed his vast ego and limited judgment before a rapt nation, it was impossible not to watch. He had organized a spectacular celebration to commemorate twenty-five hundred years of Persian empire at the ancient ruins of Persepolis, the seat of Iran's kings since before the birth of Christ. Monarchs and presidents from around the world descended on Iran for the extravaganza, designed to show off Iran's impressive progress in pursuit of modernity and global relevance, as well as its glorious past. Iranians were meant to notice how their country has ascended in the world's regard. Instead, most noticed that the shah had spent $300 million on makeshift silk tents with marble bathrooms, and on food and wine for twenty-five thousand people, flown in from Paris. The sight I could not forget was that of the Imperial Guard, dressed in costumes of the ancient soldiers of the Achaemenid empire, their beards grown long and curled elaborately. It was as though a spell had been cast, and they had unpeeled themselves from the reliefs of the ancient ruins to stride before the twentieth-century court.

Ayatollah Khomeini issued a terse condemnation from Najaf, invoking the millions of poor Iranians who he said requested the clergy's aid in building bathhouses, for they were without baths:

"The crimes of the kings of Iran have blackened the pages of history. . . . What happened to all these gilded promises, those pretentious claims . . . that the people are prosperous and content?"

Sitting there in the cool offices of the Justice Ministry, watching the television that day, I had a rare premonition. The shah's Iran, precisely like his Persepolis proceedings, was like a spellbinding evening that could not last. Like the party, it was too baroque, too alien to our reality, too magnificently ephemeral to endure. The rhetoric coming out of Najaf did not particularly capture my attention, and like most Iranians, I did not follow closely the clerical criticism of the shah. Watching it all in my office, I made no link between what transpired on the screen and where I was sitting. I did not consciously credit the shah with running an Iran in which I could be a judge, in the same way that in the revolutionary days that were to follow, I did not imagine Ayatollah Khomeini heralding an Iran in which I could not.

Though a secular government ran the country, though I was a female sitting judge with a promising career ahead of me, patriarchy still ruled Iranian culture, and it sent most of my suitors packing. Fortunately, I did not mind that being a judge seemed to complicate my marriage prospects dramatically. Law books and ideas interested me more than place settings and interior design, and my work complemented my life so richly that I didn't feel a great, aching gap that only a husband could fill.

Nevertheless, it did not escape my attention that though I came from a good family, was not bad looking, and held a respectable job, my suitors were few. Bottom line: my career struck fear in the hearts of Iranian men. The moment they thought of marrying me, they imagined themselves in a marital tiff with a judge—supposing, I assume, that they could not just say "Because I said so" and slam a door—and ran in the other direction. I found that this applied to educated, supposedly modern Iranian men as well as traditional ones; they simply preferred to be superior and more important than the women they married. And an independent woman with her own pursuits would naturally be less available to dote on them and serve them at all hours.

This revealed itself to me time and time again, and many potential suitors felt comfortable making the point explicitly, as though being a judge was a universally acknowledged deal breaker. One evening at a friend's party, a young man circled around me half the night, until he persuaded the host to introduce us. He was so sweetly persistent that when the host finally approached and asked if I was willing to meet, I said yes. It was arranged for us to meet at another party the following week. He declared himself smitten, and said that if I reciprocated his interest, he would immediately ask for my hand in marriage. Apparently, he had no idea that I was a judge. On the fateful day of the next party, he found out before greeting me, and marched up to the host, declaring that if he'd known I was judge, he would never have insisted on seeing me again.

On a chilly, clear spring morning in 1975, a young electrical engineer named Javad Tavassolian entered my courtroom and pretended to ask my opinion on some obscure legal question. He wore an elegant off-white suit over a brown shirt, its collar carefully turned out, and lingered awhile to chat. My next-door neighbor, a mutual friend, had suggested that we meet each other. I wasn't immediately attracted to him, but I was intrigued enough to agree when he suggested that we go out to dinner. After several casual meetings, chats over coffee or ice cream, he asked me to marry him. I looked at him across the table. I concentrated for a long moment, then said I couldn't give him a final answer just yet. "I have an idea," I proposed. "Why don't we spend six more months getting to know each other, and then not meet again for a month. At that month's end, we can decide whether we're actually right for each other." He agreed, and that's precisely what we did.

My parents were open-minded and believed that I should get to know a potential marriage partner well, before we locked ourselves into a future together. They let us socialize and come and go as we pleased. Two or three evenings a week, Javad and I would meet for dinner, navigating the frantically busy rush-hour traffic, to pick among the numerous European restaurants strewn across Tehran. We'd sit late after dinner, our hands circled around hot cups of tea, listening to the singers who in those days crooned in the dinner clubs of Tehran, and comparing what we wanted out of life, what an ideal future meant to us. We related to each other easily, and it felt as though I had known him much longer than a few short months. One night, at the end of our regular dinner, the waiter kept treading past our table, neglecting to bring us the bill. Javad leaned back patiently in his chair, but my eyes narrowed, and I picked up my purse. "Where are you going?" he asked. "We haven't paid yet." "This," I said, "is how you force people to pay attention to you." And I stood up and began to walk out. He hesitated a moment, then followed. Sure enough, the waiter caught up with us at the door, and apologetically handed over our check. I scanned Javad's face to see if my boldness discomfited him. He was fishing in his pockets for his keys, as though walking out had been the most natural thing in the world.

When our six months of courtship concluded, we stopped seeing each other for a month, as planned. The thirty days of distance gave us time to think. It wasn't just habit and familiarity that drew us together, we decided, but a deeper conviction that a life together would work. Javad's family drove to my parents' home in Tehran, and we performed all the traditional rites and rituals. They conducted a formal *khastegari* and asked for my hand in marriage. My family held an *aghd-konoon* at our house, and in the company of our closest friends and family, we gathered in front of the *sofreh aghd*, the traditional Iranian wedding spread. Tehran's prosecutor general was to be one of our witnesses, and he was late. As we sat awaiting his arrival, my mother had time to notice and fret that the Koran on the marriage spread was too small. At that moment, the prosecutor general arrived, bearing an elegant, nicely sized Koran as our wedding gift. A very good omen, I thought to myself, and placed the new Koran in the middle of the spread. The happily married and single women in the family (divorced women were barred by custom, lest their bitter fate bode ill for our own) held a lace canopy over our heads and ground gauze-wrapped domes of sugar into its folds, to augur sweetness in our marriage. Javad was thirty-three, and I was twenty-eight.

After an idyllic week's honeymoon in Shiraz, we returned to our new place in Tehran to start our life together. Javad owned a two-

My wedding, in 1975.

story home in Niavaran, in north Tehran. Today, grotesque custard-colored apartment towers scale the north of the city well above Niavaran, and the traffic clogs its streets as relentlessly as it does the rest of the city; but back then it was a sparsely populated area, still mostly orchards, far from the city's center. We decided to rent that house out and lease an apartment in Amirabad, near my family.

When we moved in, I hadn't realized that the ground floor of the modest, three-story building was occupied by a supreme court justice. The judge, however, had inquired about his new neighbors, and he knocked on our door as I was deciding how to arrange the sofas. He was an august, round man with overgrown whiskers, and he carried as a housewarming present a book on how to avoid marital conflict, which he had written. Leaning against the door frame, he dispensed some verbal advice as well. "You must," he said very seriously, "guard against the creep of rancor into your marriage. Try always to resolve your conflicts before they degenerate into fights, where you both vent at each other's expense." I thanked him very politely. A couple of nights later, through the open window, I heard a loud crash, followed by what sounded like the enraged screech of a large cat. After those initial volleys, an angry voice, unmistakably belonging to the judge, let out a torrent of abuse, returned with equal violence by his wife. Even after I shut the window, their shouting reverberated through the apartment. Perhaps I should go down and loan him his own book, I thought mischievously.

On our fourth or fifth evening in our new apartment, at about ten-thirty, we heard a loud knock at the door. Javad opened it to find a handful of my university friends, holding flowers. They wanted to see whether I would behave as the Shirin of old or like a newly married woman. In traditional Iranian marriages, wives often stop socializing with their old friends with spontaneous informality; husbands treat their homes as private castles, where they leave the world outside behind and enter a sanctum dedicated to their comfort. Straggling late-night friends are not meant to cross the moat. Unsure what

Javad's reaction would be, I glanced nervously at him. He seemed genuinely happy, and graciously swept them inside.

Javad came from a conservative social background, but he was as flexible and tolerant as most men of that tradition were demanding and rigid. He let me be myself from the beginning, and encouraged my work as a part of me, rather than as a hobby or an indulgence. After my father, he was the second central man in my life who tried to strengthen, rather than inhibit, my independence. None of that means that I did not have to fulfill the age-old social contract between Iranian husbands and wives. I opened up room in my cluttered schedule to stop at the produce stand, filling bags with herbs and fruit to stock our kitchen. Cleaning? That was my task, of course, as was balancing our checkbook. There was no such thing as division of household responsibilities, really, as all the tasks, from cooking to cleaning to paperwork, were mine alone. I didn't hold this against him; that's just the way it was. I recognized fairly early on that I could not have everything. That Javad championed my career was itself tremendous; if the balance of household work swung entirely in my direction, that was a compromise I was willing to make.

As I watched my girlfriends from the university take on jobs and find partners, my own choices and the compromises they entailed seemed even more right to me. Most of us had gone on to work, and in this I was in no sense an anomaly. Of my close circle of friends, only one, whom I will call Roya, put her career aside for her marriage. Roya, with her arresting mane of auburn hair and her refined tastes, attracted the attentions of a wealthy young engineer shortly after our graduation. In his eyes, a woman should work only if her husband's income was not ample enough to provide a comfortable lifestyle for both of them. Since he was so well off, he saw no need for Roya to work, and he discouraged her from becoming a judge, as the rest of us had done. She thought that if she tried to persuade him gingerly, over time he would consent to letting her work, realizing that she wanted a job to enrich her person, not their bank account. I suggested that she apply for a license to practice law, so that if he changed his mind she would be in a position to begin working right away. She acquired her license, his opinion stayed fixed, and her career never even began.

Two of my other close girlfriends, Maryam and Sara, married men who coped well with their professional ambitions. Maryam was my particular intimate. We were both passionate about becoming judges, and spent hours together debating fine points of the law. She was my sounding board for the journal articles I had begun to write, and she shared my aspirations of making as wide a contribution as our judgeship would allow. Sara, unlike Maryam and me, had a scholar's temperament. The intricacy of legal regimes fascinated her the same way the dynamism of the legal process drew us, and in her bookishness she found soporific subjects such as trade law riveting. When we graduated she started working as a researcher at the law faculty and fell in love with a junior professor. She continued working after their marriage, and all of us, save Roya the housewife, still had plenty to talk about when we gathered our university circle together for dinner.

One morning in the fall of 1977, I looked up from my desk in the courtroom to see a leaflet sitting on my files. Addressed to the shah, it warned him that he was overstepping the powers allotted him by the constitution, and that as a monarch he should not interfere with the government's affairs. The words belonged to the deposed and deceased prime minister Mossadegh. I picked up the leaflet and scanned the signatures. Among them was that of Dariush Forouhar, a trial lawyer. I didn't know it then, but in the years to come I would see his name on many files, some more ominous than I had the power then to imagine. The offices of the ministry buzzed with talk of the leaflet. I was not sure what it meant, that such a declaration had made its way into the halls of government. I just remember being impressed with

Me a few years after I became a judge.

the daring of the signatories, to challenge a reigning monarch with the fighting words of the prime minister he had deposed.

The atmosphere in the streets of Tehran was shifting too. Before the accelerated pace of events began making headlines in the newspapers, they were evident in my world of the judiciary. Sometime after the passing of the leaflet, the shah's regime tried to reduce the jurisdictional power of the court by setting up the so-called Mediating Council, an extrajudicial outfit that would have adjudicated cases outside the formal justice system. Some of the justices wrote a protest letter arguing against the council, and demanding that all cases had to be tried before a court of law. It was the first collective action taken by the judges, and it generated loud controversy. I signed the protest letter, as the matter seemed fairly straightforward to me—of course you could not entrust justice to some ad hoc council. The signatories of the letter were threatened with expulsion from the courts, but nothing came of the threat, and we proceeded with work as usual.

The shah's regime had far more to worry about than the polite protest letter of a handful of judges. In January 1978, President Jimmy Carter arrived in Tehran on a New Year's Day visit and called Iran "an island of stability." The evening news broadcast footage of the shah toasting Carter with champagne, the first time a largely Muslim nation had observed their leader drinking alcohol on national television. Not long after, a newspaper published an article aggressively attacking Ayatollah Khomeini. The next day, seminarians in the holy city of Qom revolted, marching on the shrine with chants calling for the ayatollah's return. The police shot into the crowd, and a number of men were killed.

There was no precise moment when I stopped and discerned the broad outlines of what was taking shape before me. There was no obvious signal that the fracas was more than overheated politics, that it was an unfolding revolution under the banner of Islam. The intervention of mullahs in Iranian politics was a historical phenomenon, as much of the ages as of the late 1970s. In 1906, for example, the mullahs lent their critical support to a movement that produced the Constitutional Revolution, which forced the reigning dynasty to decree a European-style constitution and legislative body into existence. For much of the previous two centuries, public space had been centered on the mosque and the bazaar. The mosque in particular offered a public gathering place where grievances against the moment's king could be freely aired and exchanged, behind the semiprotected walls of a holy building. Our history was dotted with such fruitful illustrations of the mullahs' intervention, and so to the ears of ordinary Iranians, myself included, it was neither shocking nor particularly foreboding to hear Ayatollah Khomeini raining invective down on the shah from exile.

*B*y the summer of 1978, the mood had turned thoroughly vicious; the protests grew larger and larger, and it was no longer possible to sit on the fence, observing the confrontations that were roiling the country. In early August, a crowded cinema in the southern city of Abadan was burned to the ground. The flames engulfed four hundred people, burning them alive. The shah blamed religious conservatives, and Ayatollah Khomeini angrily accused the SAVAK, the regime's secret police, by then a force legendary for its brutality against the government's opponents.

The tragic fire convinced many Iranians that the shah was not simply an American puppet fumbling the nation's interests but a malignant despot willing to sacrifice the lives of the ordinary to cling to his throne. I realized only two decades later the momentous power of such a moment—how an egregious act can electrify a population until then ambivalent, and convince them that a confined dispute between political forces carried implications worthy of drawing them out of their living rooms, into the fray. A month later, at the end of the fasting month of Ramadan, one hundred thousand people poured into the streets, the first of the grand marches against the shah. An ocean of Iranians as far as the eye could see filled the wide boulevards of Tehran and raised their voices against the shah.

I found myself drawn to the opposition voices that hailed Ayatollah Khomeini as their leader. It seemed in no way a contradiction for me—an educated, professional woman—to back an opposition that cloaked its fight against real-life grievances under the mantle of religion. Faith occupied a central role in our middle-class lives, though in a quiet, private way; my mother had spent hours bent over the *jah-namaz* teaching me how to pray, and my father encouraged me to recite my prayers throughout my life. Who did I have more in common with, in the end: an opposition led by mullahs who spoke in the tones familiar to ordinary Iranians or the gilded court of the shah, whose officials cavorted with American starlets at parties soaked in expensive French champagne? Obviously not the court, whose loyalists basically included only courtiers, some top officials, and families enriched by business ties to the regime. Most of the country identified far more with the opposition, which included secular nationalists, socialists, and Marxists among its ranks. Among these opposition groups, the mullahs' voices were the loudest; it was the clergy, whose network of mosques spread out across the country, who had standing centers from which to raise their voices and organize. It did not seem so alarming that the mullahs should take the lead.

As the days went by, the fervor touched everyone around me, and we all looked for ways to participate. One morning, Ayatollah Khomeini issued a statement instructing people to expel the ministers from their offices in the ministries. Several judges and officials in the court gathered together in the hallway, and I joined them. We collected ourselves, managed to fire one another up a bit, and barged into the minister of justice's office. The minister was out, and one of the elder judges was sitting behind one of the desks. He looked up at us in amazement, and his gaze halted when he saw my face. "*You!* You of all people, why are you here?" he asked, bewildered and stern. "Don't you know that you're supporting people who will take your job away if they come to power?" "I'd rather be a free Iranian than an enslaved attorney," I retorted boldly, self-righteous to the core. Years later, whenever we ran into each other, he would remind me of that fateful remark.

After that morning, the heated debates in the ministry usually occurred in my office, and as I was a female judge, my pro-revolutionary sympathies were especially welcomed. One day we all signed a poetic letter to the president of France, after the ayatollah took up exile there and continued his refrain of "The shah must go!" from Paris, instead of Najaf. On another symbolic afternoon we decided to take down the shah's picture in the ministry. The shah had not yet fled, and it was not altogether clear that he would. A group of us gathered and approached the photo—the shah's regal, vacant expression staring down at us from the wall—while a number of colleagues stood between us and the portrait, pleading for us to leave it in its place. Yet another day the ministry staff staged a strike and brought the court's operation to a standstill. Even during the strike, I was so captivated by the revolutionary atmosphere that I continued going to work, simply to be there and lend my support.

The unfolding revolution hypnotized me, but most fascinating of all were the turncoats, the overnight switching of allegiances. In those days, the base opportunism of human nature, the willingness to abandon and take on ideology as though it were a coat, was everywhere on display. The judges and ministry staff notorious for their collaboration with the shah's regime, and especially with the SAVAK, monitored the temperature of public sentiment closely, and when it became clear that the revolution could not be turned back—when the marches swelled to two million people and lasted hours on end—they joined the ranks of the revolutionaries.

On January 16, 1979, a bitterly cold winter day, the shah fled Iran, carrying with him a small box of Iranian soil. When he fled, he ended two millennia of rule by Persian kings. People filled the streets, celebrating. I dressed quickly and drove over to my parents' house, to pick up my mother and sister. We tied two handkerchiefs to the windshield wipers; they blew back and forth as if held by the arms of a dancing robot, as we drove out to join the crowd, swept up by its euphoria. We felt as though we had reclaimed a dignity that, until recently, many of us had not even realized we had lost.

On February 1, 1979, the heavy-lidded, stern face of Ayatollah Khomeini emerged from an Air France jetliner, and the imam slowly stepped down onto the tarmac of Mehrabad Airport, ending his exile just sixteen days after the shah's began. My whole family plus a few friends sat riveted around our living room television, watching the proceedings, which seemed even more spectacular for being one of the first broadcasts we saw in color. The *chelo-kabob*, beef skewers with rice, we had ordered for lunch cooled as we followed the broadcaster onto the imam's plane. How do you feel today, upon returning to Iran after such a long exile? he was asked. We leaned in closely. "I have no feeling," he replied, expressionless.

"What a ridiculous question!" a friend exclaimed. "He's the leader of a revolution, not a film star on the red carpet." "But how can someone spend fourteen years in exile," interrupted his wife, "return under these unbelievable circumstances, and say 'I have no feeling?'" The camera pulled back to show the streets clogged with millions of celebrating Iranians honking horns, ecstatic at the return of the seventy-eight-year-old ayatollah. Suddenly, the broadcast cut out, and the screen went black. My father threw his hands in the air, crying, "It's a coup d'état!" For a second, we all sat back in terror, imagining that the ayatollah had been killed, imagining the streets would be filled with blood.

The army was still loyal to the shah, and the previous day the Imperial Guard had sent battle tanks and troop-filled trucks into the streets of Tehran to show that they would not surrender the reins of power so quickly. Columns of tanks over a mile long crawled through the city, razing barricades and firing on demonstrators who blocked the way.

We called every revolutionary friend we could think of, but their phones just rang. We sat there festering with anxiety, until a cousin drove out into the streets and came back with reports that everyone was still celebrating. Ayatollah Khomeini did not speak that day of an Islamic state, nor did he say what would come next. But he called on God to cut off the hands of Iran's enemies.

For about a month, the country hung in the balance. In most cities, an emergency military government had gone into effect, and the ayatollah ordered people back into their homes by nightfall. He instructed the nation to march up to their rooftops en masse at nine P.M. and scream *Allaho akbar*, God is greatest. It was an ingenious way to harness the momentum of the marches, to literally raise the volume of fury and discontent, without lining people up to be shot in the streets. More than any other, this tactic revealed how effectively the ayatollah was able to play on the religious emotionalism of the masses in his campaign against the shah.

Each evening, my husband and I climbed the stairs to our roof and dutifully bellowed *Allaho akbar* for a full half hour, until we were hoarse. I remember gazing out across the rooftops of the city, people milling atop the low-rise buildings for as far as the eye could see, turning their heads to the night sky so their voices could rise. The gorgeous, hymnal air of these lofted cries hung over the stilled city, so spiritually enchanting that even my stolid, cynical friends were moved.

One morning during the months of *Allaho akbar*, my mother and I ran into a neighbor at the bank. My mother, usually charming and in command of herself in company, began explaining in an odd, forceful manner that because she and my father were elderly, it was hard for them to scale the steep stairs to the roof. "Instead," she said, "we shout *Allaho akbar* from our bedroom window." I sensed that she was embarrassed before the neighbors, being unable to climb to her roof and join her voice to the neighborhood's cries. "Maman," I interrupted, "it's all right; I yell for you as well."

In those days, if a house remained dark and its roof empty, everyone wondered why. Today, when the government orders people out onto their roofs on the twenty-second of Bahman, in memory of those nights, only a few houses emit cries of *Allaho akbar*, rather plaintively, and now no one wonders why.

The military, holding its ground, had imposed a four P.M. curfew on the country. On February 11, Ayatollah Khomeini exhorted people to defy the curfew and come out onto the streets. I went outside that day, the shots of gunfire echoing through the streets, and watched people attack police stations. Many of the soldiers and police officers simply dissolved into the crowd, joining multitudes who embraced them in scenes of frenzied emotion, distributing their caches of firearms among the populace. Only a few soldiers and officers held back, and the shots we heard were their last volleys of resistance. The next day, the twenty-second of Bahman on the Iranian calendar, the military commanders issued a statement declaring that the armed forces would not take sides and would remain on their bases. This meant the military had surrendered, and that evening the prime minister fled his office, and then the country. State television and radio went dead, and then a scratchy, tremulous voice came on, announcing that the state media had been taken over by the people.

Ever since that day, the twenty-second of Bahman has been celebrated as the date of the revolution's victory. In Persian, we do not say the revolution was born, that it happened or came to pass; we require an oversize verb, and so we say the revolution was victorious. That day, a feeling of pride washed over me that in hindsight makes me laugh. I felt that I too had won, alongside this victorious revolution. It took scarcely a month for me to realize that, in fact, I had willingly and enthusiastically participated in my own demise. I was a woman, and this revolution's victory demanded my defeat.

CHAPTER THREE

The Bitter Taste of Revolution

THE HEAD-SCARF "INVITATION" WAS THE FIRST WARNING that this revolution might eat its sisters, which was what women called one another while agitating for the shah's overthrow. Imagine the scene, just days after the revolution's victory. A man named Fathollah Bani-Sadr was appointed provisional overseer of the Ministry of Justice. Still flush with pride, a group of us chose a clear, breezy afternoon to descend on his office and congratulate him. We filed into the room, and many warm greetings and flowery congratulations were exchanged. Then Bani-Sadr's eyes fell on me. I expected he might thank me, or express how much it meant to him that a committed female judge such as myself had stood with the revolution.

Instead, he said, "Don't you think that out of respect for our beloved Imam Khomeini, who has graced Iran with his return, it would be better if you covered your hair?" I was shaken. Here we were, in the Ministry of Justice, after a great popular revolt had replaced an antique monarchy with a modern republic, and the new overseer of justice was talking about hair. Hair!

"I've never worn a head scarf in my life," I said, "and it would be hypocritical to start now."

"So don't be a hypocrite, and wear it with belief!" he said, as though he had just solved my dilemma.

"Look, don't be glib," I replied. "I shouldn't be forced to wear a veil, and if I don't believe in it, I'm just not going to wear one."

"Don't you see how the situation is developing?" he asked, his voice rising.

"Yes, but I don't want to pretend to be something I'm not," I said. And then I left the room.

I didn't want to hear, or even think about, the kind of reality "the situation" had in store for us. I was distracted with more intimate concerns. That spring, after a second miscarriage the previous year, Javad and I had planned a trip to New York to visit a fertility specialist. The appointments had been made long in advance, before the massive breakdown in social order, and now traveling was nearly impossible. Everyone, by decree, was *mamnoo ol-khorooj*, barred from leaving the country. I appealed to Abbas Amir-Entezam, the deputy prime minister, with a special letter from the head prosecutor's office. Amir-Entezam—who was shortly thereafter arrested, and is *still* serving prison time to this day—granted us permission, and in April we flew to the United States. Tehran's Mehrabad Airport, usually bustling with passengers on flights to Europe, felt like something between a ghost town and a military base. Our bags were searched minutely, lest they be full of antiques or illicit government cash, and we boarded the Boeing along with the fifteen other passengers on the flight. As we stretched out in the empty rows, I gazed out the window at the Tehran disappearing beneath us, and wondered what sort of Iran we would find upon our return.

The specialists in New York were sympathetic. And perhaps in those days also more frank about what advanced medicine could do for a woman in her thirties struggling to conceive. There was an Iranian gynecologist among the Long Island clinic's fertility team, and he put it to me, in a classically Persian way, with a metaphor about blossoms: "An apple tree might grow a hundred buds, but all of them don't turn into apples. Can we explain why, with the same watering and climate, some of the buds fall, and others turn into fruit? Certainly not." He explained that doctors simply cannot detect the cause of some miscarriages, and that I should fight back the depression and keep trying.

The day after we flew back to Tehran, I went straight to work. We had been gone for less than a month, but it was already a different city. The streets that crisscrossed Tehran—long boulevards with names like Eisenhower, Roosevelt, Queen Elizabeth, and Peacock Throne—had been renamed after Shia imams, martyred clerics, and Third World heroes of anti-imperial struggle. During our short absence, people had begun wearing their support for the revolution on their sleeves, literally. As my taxi crept past government buildings in downtown Tehran, I noticed that the usual line of ministry cars along the curb was missing, and a long line of motorcycles was parked in their stead. When I arrived at the court, I passed from hall to hall, peeking incredulously into various offices. The men were no longer wearing suits and ties but plain slacks and collarless shirts, many of them quite wrinkled, some even stained. Even my nose caught a whiff of the change. The slight scent of cologne or perfume that had lingered in the corridors, especially in the mornings, was absent. Finding one of my female colleagues in the hall, I whispered my shock at the overnight transformation, as though the ministry staff were in dress rehearsal for a play about urban poverty.

At some moment during my short absence, apparently the populist revolt had stopped to devote attention to truly consequential matters, such as the outlawing of the tie on government property. The radical mullahs had long disparaged Westernized technocrats as *fokoli*, from the French word *faux-col*, or bow tie, and now the tie was deemed a symbol of the West's evils, smelling of cologne signaled counterrevolutionary tendencies, and riding the ministry car to work was evidence of class privilege. In the new atmosphere, everyone aspired to appear poor, and the wearing of dirty clothes had become a mark of political integrity, a sign of one's sympathy with the dispossessed.

"What are these chairs!" Ayatollah Taleghani, one of the prominent revolutionary clerics, had famously barked in complaint after arriving to rewrite the constitution at the senate building and finding a roomful of elegant brocaded chairs. They were already here, his aides said defensively; we didn't go out and buy them or anything. For days, the ayatollah and his assembly penned the constitution while sitting cross-legged on the floor, until they gave up and perched on the corrupt chairs.

There was truly an air of theater to those times, but I was distracted by the rumors swirling through the judiciary, rumors so appalling that with each new repeating, I had to breathe in gulps of air to beat back my despair. The word in the halls was that Islam barred women from being judges. I tried to laugh these rumors off. I counted many senior revolutionaries among my friends, and reasoned that my connections were strong. I should mention, only for the sake of communicating what my potential removal could symbolize, that I was the most distinguished female judge in the Tehran court. My published articles had secured me some exposure, and beyond that, I had loaned the credential of my support—the support of a top female judge—to the revolution. Surely, I thought to myself, they will not come for me. If they came for me, it meant it was all over for women in the justice system, and perhaps in the government altogether.

For several months, during which I became pregnant, I stood my ground. One day, the provisional justice minister Bani-Sadr, he of the head-scarf invitation, summoned me to his office and suggested gently that he transfer me to the investigative office of the ministry. It would have been a prestigous job, but I worried that my stepping down would carry implications, and people would presume that the ranks of judgeship were closing to women. I said no. Bani-Sadr warned me that a purging committee might be formed, and that I could potentially be demoted to court assistant. "I'm not stepping down voluntarily," I said.

"$\mathcal{A}$ group identifying itself as Followers of the Path of the Imam Khomeini has seized the U.S. embassy, and taken its staff hostage!" the radio announced urgently one evening in early November 1979 as I stood before the kitchen sink, five months pregnant, rinsing fresh herbs for dinner. The group's name seemed oddly meaningless to me. At the time, everyone followed in the path of Imam Khomeini, and if they didn't, they dared not say so. I put the colander aside and immediately thought of the Vienna Convention on Consular Relations. What thoughtless radicals these young people must be, I said to myself. How on earth can you take diplomats hostage? I imagined that America would surely be enraged at this hostile takeover and proceed to attack Iran, in its postrevolutionary disarray in no position to defend itself. I expected Ayatollah Khomeini, if for no other reason than to fend off an American strike, to command these kids (and they really were just kids; if you saw their faces on the nightly news, you saw immediately that they were barely twenty) to release the hostages. A few days passed. Not only did he not order their release, but he praised their bravery. And America did not attack. It said only that it would freeze Iranian assets in the United States, which struck me as very strange, as though America viewed cash as tactically symmetrical: you take our diplomats hostage, we take your cash hostage.

When I think back to these times, my own naïveté astounds me. The ethics of the matter seemed so blindingly simple. Hostage taking contravenes international law. It is illegal, and therefore wrong and to be condemned. Why was it happening? My fog of bewilderment reminds me of Amir Abbas Hoveyda, a prime minister who served the shah for fourteen years in that office and was thrown in prison by the disloyal monarch the last year before the revolution, an all-too-late human sacrifice meant to stanch people's rising discontent. On the day of the revolution, Hoveyda's prison guards deserted their posts and suggested that he flee as well. Staunch in his belief that he had done nothing wrong, Hoveyda saw no reason to flee like a common criminal. He stayed put, imagining that a fair trial would soon be convened to establish his innocence. Like me, he was surely familiar with the history of great revolutions, the textbook accounts of the French and Bolshevik revolts that resulted in heads being paraded around on stakes. But also like me, his perception of the world could not admit the rage and tumult inherent in the violent overthrow of an entrenched order. Perhaps we were too overwhelmed by the sight of our own Tehran collapsing around us to realize that rules and justice would be lost in the chaos, as is the case with all revolutions. What was he thinking? What was I thinking? Did he really believe they would pause in their frenzy, cancel their million-person marches, and hold a fair, air-conditioned trial with a court transcriber for him? Did I really believe that the armed twenty-year-olds drunk on power at the U.S. embassy would leaf through the Vienna Convention and change their minds? Neither of us had absorbed the revolution, really. What idiots we were.

Once Ayatollah Khomeini celebrated the siege, calling it a "second revolution," no one dared contradict him in public. Many Iranians were deeply opposed to the taking of hostages, but they said nothing outside their homes, fearful of being accused of being an American agent and sentenced to prison. The supporters of the siege gave no thought to Iran's reputation in the world. The ayatollah had said, "America cannot do a damn thing," and this slogan was soon painted all over Tehran. A deceptive pride held people enthralled. They thought that by successfully taking the U.S. embassy hostage, they had defeated America.

I can say with reasonable certainty that Iranians nervous about the Vienna Convention implications of the hostage crisis numbered in the minority. Most Iranians, under the spell of the ayatollah's unparalleled charisma, considered the students heroes.

The siege of the embassy swiftly became the central drama of the revolution. The students announced that they had unearthed classified intelligence documents and began issuing statements naming Iranians who had allegedly spied for the American government. With each new statement, these student hostage takers effectively signed the death warrants of the alleged collaborators. People converged on the embassy in a frenzy of excitement, filling the busy intersections around the expansive complex and screaming, "Death to America." Callow militants patrolled the grounds, which were about the size of a small junior college campus, complete with tennis courts, gardens, and a giant auditorium—an embassy whose very size reflected the intimate relations between the U.S. government and the shah's Iran.

One afternoon a friend of mine phoned to ask if I wanted to go to the embassy. "Will they let us inside?" I asked. "No, but there are big crowds," she said. "I think it'd be amusing to stroll around." By that time food vendors hawking steamed beets, roast corn, cold soda, and all sorts of Iranian snack foods had lined up their carts along the streets around the embassy, as though it were a picnic grounds. Parents brought children in strollers, young children licked ice-cream cones, and the devoted bought portraits of the ayatollah along with their fresh melon juice. Basically, what had started out as a sit-in turned into a traumatic international rupture, and both then turned into a street fair. "Sorry," I told my friend, "I'm not interested in folly as spectator sport." Night after night, the television broadcast these young people's press releases and scenes from the omnipresent crowds. The siege lasted longer than any of us could have imagined, 444 days in total. I remember how half the world sent envoys to Ayatollah Khomeini, pleading with him to release the hostages. Even the pope sent someone. "On behalf of the pope, in the name of humanity," the envoy beseeched, "please let them go." "Where was the pope," the ayatollah replied, unmoved, "when our young people were being tortured in the shah's prisons?"

Many of the Islamic Republic's future politicians emerged from the group that took the embassy hostage, which called itself Students Following the Imam's Line. From well-known hard-liners to leading reformist figures, the hostage takers filled the ranks of government, though their hero status in the eyes of most Iranians sank in the years to come, especially once the war with Iraq ended and people began feeling the scale of the damage the siege had wrought on Iran's place in the world. The fall of the Soviet Union produced a unipolar global order, and enmity with the world's only and great superpower carried serious burdens. The long arm of the economic sanctions the United States imposed meant that Iran could not avail itself of American contractors to maintain its oil infrastructure, built entirely by American firms. It could no longer buy Boeing aircraft or service the fleet of Boeings it already owned, and eventually even the European Airbus—on account of its American-made engine—became off-limits. Iran's fleet of civilian aircraft decayed with each passing year, and the government began buying Russian-made Tupolevs, which plummeted from the sky with alarming regularity. Even today, if you ride an Iran Air flight to Europe, you might find yourself on an antique Boeing 747 from the 1970s, a lone relic from an era when the Iranian ambassador to Washington threw the most famous parties in the U.S. capital, and the American ambassador to Tehran hosted Bloody Mary brunches.

The hostage taking intertwined the fates of the United States and Iran for decades to come, though it was perhaps the last time the two nations faced off directly. A revolutionary Iran continued to target Americans in the chaos of early 1980s Beirut, sending its radicals and Revolutionary Guards to Lebanon, a small Mediterranean country embroiled in civil strife, to start up the Shia militant group Hezbollah. In the spring of 1983, a suicide bomber drove a pickup truck with explosives into the U.S. embassy in Beirut, killing sixty-three people; in the fall of the same year, another suicide bombing at a U.S. military barracks in Beirut killed 241 marines. After successfully introducing the suicide car bomb as a weapon in urban combat, Islamic extremists reportedly backed by Iran began kidnapping Americans, including a CIA station chief; their captors were linked to the Iranian Revolutionary Guards, and the diplomats who sought to free them flew to Tehran to negotiate.

On the face of things, hostility reigned between the United States and Iran, with the latter striking out against its newly perceived foe on the distant battlefield of the Levantine capital. But even from the Iranian end of the hostage siege, rumors swirled of secret backdoor contacts between the public foes. Senior members of President Jimmy Carter's outgoing administration alleged that the hostage takers had agreed through private channels to delay the hostages' release until the day of President Reagan's inauguration. And indeed, only hours after Reagan was sworn in, he informed the nation that the siege had ended.

The Iran-Contra scandal of the mid-1980s fueled these suspicions, when it was leaked that the United States was selling Iran missiles in exchange for the release of hostages. The scandal tarnished the Reagan administration, but it also made Iranians permanently question their government's fiery anti-American stance, especially when details of a secret mission to Iran emerged: in 1986, President Reagan dispatched national security adviser Robert McFarlane to Tehran bearing a now-notorious chocolate cake in the shape of a key and a Bible with an inscription in the president's own hand. The key-shaped cake went down as political legend in Iran, a frosted symbol of the private cooperation behind the two nations' public antagonism.

The 444-day hostage siege was no pedestrian confrontation between two sovereign states. The clichéd wisdom in Washington understands the relationship as a marriage gone bad, in which high emotions figure as importantly as strategic calculations in both parties' dealings. This perspective conveniently understands Iran's behavior as a flare-up of radical Islam against the secular shah. But in Iran, collective memory extends further back, and the opening salvos are dated to 1953, when an America coup removed Mossadegh from power.

Many of the hostage takers, along with revolutionary figures, underwent an intellectual transformation in the 1990s. They concluded that the revolution had veered off course, lost sight of its ideal of freedom and independence, and was alienating Iranians with its own rampant corruption and repressiveness. They helped pioneer a reform movement in the late 1990s of regime insiders seeking to check the Islamic Republic's authoritarian ways. When, in 2001, the grounds of the U.S. embassy were opened to the public for the first time with a macabre exhibit dedicated to "America's crimes around the world"—complete with devil-horned effigies of Uncle Sam and a Statue of Liberty with a live dove encased in her stomach—they refused to attend.

The meeting in which I was stripped of my judgeship took place in a large room in the district court, in the final days of 1980. It was more a dismissal, really, than a meeting, because the men on the purging committee didn't even offer me a seat. They sat behind a wooden table. Two of them were judges I knew well, one of whom until the previous year had been my junior. I stubbornly kept standing, my hands grasping a seat back; I was six months pregnant, and I wondered whether they would at least be decent enough to suggest I sit down. One of them picked up a sheet of paper and rudely tossed it toward me across the table.

"Show up to the legal office when you're done with your vacation," he said brusquely. The "legal office" was where the judiciary clerks reported. "Show up to the legal office" meant I was being demoted to a clerk, a paper pusher, a typist.

No one else said a word. I looked at the two judges I knew, who sat flanking the head purger.

"Without even starting at the legal office, she wants a vacation," the head purger said.

At this point I knew he was purposely trying to provoke me, so I ran my hand over my distended belly and said that maternity leave was guaranteed by employment law.

And then the unthinkable occurred. They began speaking about women judges as though I were not in the room. "They're disorganized!" one said. "Distracted constantly," another murmured. "Yes!" chimed another. "They're so unmotivated; it's obvious they don't even want to be working."

I pulled my shoulders back, cradled my stomach with a protective arm, and strode out of the room, unsure whether I could speak through my rage.

Even today, when I think about that meeting or tell the story, I can't remember how I got myself home. I must have walked, because when I showed up at the house I had clearly fallen along the way, though I don't remember falling. I don't remember crossing the busy intersections or hearing the whir of the gasping old Paykans. I didn't even open the door with my own key, but rang the doorbell and just stood on the stoop. My sister found me there, pale and expressionless, and gasped at the blood trickling down my leg, the rip in my pants. I looked down and saw the angry red gash across my knee. It was only when she hugged me close that I began to weep.

*I*n the days that followed, the unthinkable continued to occur with astonishing regularity. If I haven't mentioned it explicitly, you have probably noticed that I am stubborn. I refused to sit at home and let my personhood at the ministry simply melt away. I showed up at the legal office punctually at nine in the morning, the domain to which I had been shamefully "transferred." But from the first day I arrived there, I announced that since I had been demoted against my will, I refused to do any work, as a show of protest. The head of the legal office knew me from before and understood why I was rejecting all work. He let me be. Each day, I went to the office and simply sat in my room. The hours blurred into days, and the days into weeks.

One afternoon, a group of people showed up at the ministry and took up position outside the office of Bani-Sadr, who by that time had been appointed prosecutor general. The men belonged to an *an-joman-e Islami*, one of the many mushrooming Islamic societies that took it upon themselves to safeguard the purity of the revolution. When Bani-Sadr finally arrived, they blocked him from entering his office. They argued loudly, telling him he was not a true Islamic revolutionary; essentially, they delivered to him the same message he had delivered to me when he'd asked me to cover my hair out of deference to Ayatollah Khomeini.

Bani-Sadr stalked out of the ministry. Sometime later, once his brother had become president of Iran, he invited me to work as legal counselor at the president's office. It was an appealing offer, certainly more engaging than sitting day after day in the legal office, staring at the wall. But I declined. I had seen how fragile these political alliances could be, how the capricious revolutionaries reinvented their standards day by day. How someone who was one day lecturing others on sufficient revolutionary spirit could the next be tossed out of his office by those even more radical. I was not wrong. The man who accepted that position was executed by firing squad, when President Bani-Sadr was removed from office.

On one of the blindingly same days in the legal office, before boredom threatened to drive me mad and I gave up my strike, I read a spectacular piece of news in *Enghelab-e Eslami*, the daily newspaper called, rather unoriginally, Islamic Revolution. When I first skimmed the headline and read the draft of the Islamic penal code printed below, I was convinced I was hallucinating. How could this be? I thought. The imposition of Islamic penal code, inspired by Islamic law, is a momentous overhaul in how a society is governed. It would fundamentally transform the very basis of governance, the relationship of citizens to laws, the organizing principles and social contracts along which society is conducted. It would be a shift of such overarching significance that it should be read from the ramparts and put to the ballot. It should not, I reasoned, simply show up one day in the morning newspaper. I moved my cup of tea over on the desk, spread out the newspaper carefully, and began rereading from the top.

The grim statutes that I would spend the rest of my life fighting stared back at me from the page: the value of a woman's life was half that of a man (for instance, if a car hit both on the street, the cash compensation due to the woman's family was half that due the man's); a woman's testimony in court as a witness to a crime counted only half as much as a man's; a woman had to ask her husband's permission for divorce. The drafters of the penal code had apparently consulted the seventh century for legal advice. The laws, in short, turned the clock back fourteen hundred years, to the early days of Islam's spread, the days when stoning women for adultery and chopping off the hands of thieves were considered appropriate sentences.

I felt my body become hot and prickly with a boundless rage. A dull pain began to twitch in one of my temples, and within an hour it had grown into an excruciating, lopsided throb. I took the first of my many migraines home and lay on my bed for hours, the curtains pulled. Javad was in Europe for a few months for a training course. At least I didn't have to face cooking anything, or even setting the table. By that time, it was becoming apparent to educated Iranians that the revolution was veering in a vicious direction. Not only were the sympathies that had brought us out into the streets absent in many of the revolutionary processes under way, but there was an appetite for violence that seemed only to grow.

When the sun set and the cacophony of the evening traffic died down, when it approached nine P.M. and Tehran stilled itself, I crawled out of bed and made a cold compress to hold against my forehead. I carried a plate of biscuits into the living room and turned the television on low. I couldn't really eat; I just played with the crumbs along the plate's rim. Ayatollah Khomeini's severe face appeared on the screen, and I turned up the volume, even though the noise was nearly unbearable. In his speech, in that characteristic monotone in which he'd toppled a king and reset the course of Iranian history, he said that anyone opposing the code was against Islam and would be punished. The precedent was set in those early days: criticism was the work of the "enemies," an expanding list that included all those deemed "against Islam" and "counterrevolutionary." The lines in the sand that defined those terms were smudged out and redrawn each day. And those who ended up on the wrong side faced, as often as not, the firing squad.

Several days later, a group of law professors from Tehran University wrote a protest letter arguing that the new penal code was inappropriate to the twentieth century and should not be implemented. They were swiftly expelled from their jobs, suspended until the ensuing shortage of professors caused them to be gradually summoned back to work.

I prepared myself for all the possible ways the imposition of Islamic law could affect my life. I thought of all the ways it would make a difference: the courtrooms in which I could no longer preside, the ministry it would fill with clerics, the religious books I would now use as legal references. But in all my anxious speculation, I never imagined that fear of a new legal regime, albeit a catastrophic one, would follow me into my living room, into my marriage. Yet there was no use denying it. Ever since I'd read about the new penal code in the newspaper, I'd been behaving differently with Javad. It was as though I was wearing my skin inside out. The smallest perceived slight or off-tone remark set me on the war path or, as the Persian expression goes, guarding my front. I couldn't help it.

The day Javad and I married each other, we joined our lives together as two equal individuals. But under these laws, he stayed a person and I became chattel. They permitted him to divorce me at whim, take custody of our future children, acquire three wives and stick them in the house with me. Although I knew rationally that inside Javad lurked no such potential monster, just waiting to break out and steal our hypothetical children and marry up a storm, I still felt oppressed. A couple of weeks into the new sullen, defensive person I had become, I decided that Javad and I should have a talk.

"Listen, I just can't deal with this anymore," I told him.

"We don't have any problems," he said. And he was right. Before all of this, our biggest disagreement had been over household chores.

"I know," I responded, "but the law has made problems for us. We used to be equals, and now you've been promoted above me, and I just can't stand it. I really, really can't."

"So what do you want me to do?" he asked, throwing his hands up.

And then inspiration struck. I knew what he could do! He could sign a *post*nuptial agreement, granting me the right to divorce him, as well as primary custody of our future children, in the event of separation.

The next morning we rose at around eight, hurried through a breakfast of sweet tea and fresh bread, and rushed over to the local notary. I drove, as usual. Javad disliked driving in the city, while I enjoyed nothing more than fighting my way through the snarled boulevards of Tehran, weaving through the lanes and, like most others on the road, expressing my sheer frustration with life in Iran from behind the wheel. "You should've been a taxi driver," Javad always says to me. But funnily enough, I'm petrified of driving on the freeway. When we travel outside Tehran, Javad always drives. Speed terrifies me. If I drive above fifty miles per hour, I literally become dizzy.

Back when I was training for my judgeship, as part of our internship in the public prosecutor's branch we toured the city morgue. Fifteen freshly mangled bodies lay on the cold, steel slabs, waiting for autopsies. They had been riding a bus that had sped too fast, careened out of control, and crashed. From that day on, accelerating to highway speed has been out of the question for me.

When we arrived at the notary's, the man simply peered at Javad through his cola-bottle glasses as though he had gone mad. "Do you have any idea what you're doing, my good man?" he asked, perhaps assuming that Javad must be illiterate, to have been duped into wanting to sign such a contract. "Why are you doing this?"

I'll never forget Javad's reply:

"My decision is irrevocable. I want to save my life."

As we drove home, I glanced at his profile in the passenger seat and felt the unbearable heaviness of that law simply evaporate. We were back to where we were meant to be, equal. But a tiny part of me still minded very much. After all, I couldn't drag all the men of Iran down to the notary, could I?

On April 21, 1980, five years to the day after I met my husband, I gave birth to my daughter Negar. I had continued my "work" at the legal office until shortly before my labor, and I'd never imagined that my daughter would become—there is no other way to put it—the light in my ever-darkening life. In all honesty, I had not been very fond of children until I had my own. I stayed home for two months, watching this mysterious, pink little being, wiping the drool away from her mouth, and rubbing her back through the terry jumper so she would burp. I was captivated. And not only because her infant world, the soothing lullabies and the ritual preparation of her bottles, was such a respite from the ugliness outside, the executions and purges that would not abate.

After she was born, we couldn't afford a nanny. When the time

Negar, age one.

came for me to return to work, I would drop Negar off at my mother's house in the morning and pick her up on the way home.

I returned to a ministry even more fraught with fear and intimidation. Each day, it seemed, the revolutionaries passed another unjust and arbitrary law, and no one could whisper a protest, lest they be branded anti-Islamic. While my former colleagues had demoted me in stealth, by "transfer" to another division, soon a law was passed explicitly stating that only men could be judges, and that women judges must take on administrative positions. In a cruel bureaucratic shuffle, I was appointed secretary of the same court I had once presided over as judge. Of course, many of us female judges did not stay silent. We protested everywhere we could—in the halls, to our friends with revolutionary connections, to the new minister.

I personally sought out the revolutionaries I had been close to in the last days of the shah. The formerly open-minded ones who had not treated me as a second-class Iranian back when they'd sought my support in their campaign against the regime, when they'd needed me to sign their protest letters, to raid the offices of hapless royalist officials. Back then I had been a fellow *mobarez*, an equal in the struggle. I reminded them of all this and wouldn't stop pushing. *Why?* I asked insistently. *Just tell me why a woman can't be a judge? I stood with this revolution. You owe me an answer.*

You're right, of course. No one is arguing with you. Just be patient. We'll attend to your rights later, they promised. But we have more urgent problems right now. Can't you see?

I did see. And time would confirm my doubts about the revolutionaries. In their hierarchy of priorities, women's rights would forever come last. It was simply never the right time to defend women's rights. Twenty-five years later, they would dismiss my same arguments with the same answer: the revolution needs rescue. Gentlemen, I wondered, when, in your opinion, will be an auspicious time to attend to women's rights? In the afterlife?

But at the time, the country was in peril, and these flimsy defenses appeared more compelling. For on September 22, 1980, as though fate had not been sufficiently ungenerous with us, Saddam Hussein invaded Iran.

CHAPTER FOUR

Iran at War

"DID YOU HEAR THE NEWS? DID YOU HEAR? QUICK, TURN on the television," my friend said agitatedly as soon as I opened the door, pushing past me and rushing into the living room. I had no idea what she was talking about. Negar consumed my afternoons, and I had stopped listening to news, which I didn't trust. So she told me: at two P.M. Iraqi warplanes had attacked Mehrabad Airport and other locations in Tehran.

I put the kettle on the stove for tea and hurried back to the television. There was no programming, just the ominous, rousing drumbeat of a patriotic march. Occasionally a voice interrupted, asking viewers to stay tuned for an address by Ayatollah Khomeini. We did. "The Iranian people," he declared, "will defend their homeland." And that's how we realized that the war had begun. The phone rang. "Why don't you come over?" suggested my mother. "Let's be together on a night like this." Javad and I packed an overnight case and drove over, staying up late into the night, keeping vigil with the television and cracking pumpkin seeds, too anxious to sleep. I leaned out the window for some fresh air, and saw the lights on in many houses down the block.

By late that evening it became clear that Saddam Hussein had launched a full-blown invasion. First, Baghdad dispatched fighter planes to attack Iranian air bases in Tehran, as well as eight other Iranian cities. Saddam took inspiration for this tactic from the 1967 Arab-Israeli War, aiming to level the Iranian air force before it left the ground. But Iran's jets were tucked under specially fortified hangars, and within hours its F-4 Phantoms glided onto pockmarked runways and took off to attack Iraqi targets.

As the Iraqi planes rained missiles on Iranian air bases, six Iraqi army divisions rolled into Iranian territory on three fronts, advancing more than five hundred miles into Iranian soil. The northern front ran across the border post of Qasr-e-Shirin, in the mountainous northwestern province of the country, while the central front pushed across the desert plain below the Zagros Mountains. But the Iraqi army reserved its strongest forces for the south, home of the oil fields that Saddam dreamed of annexing to feed his fascist Baathist regime. Armed divisions crossed the Arvand River, heading for strategic points and military bases whose swift occupation would beat back Iranian reinforcements.

As the country sustained the attack, most of the shah's top army officers, those trained to fly the sleek fighter jets the shah had purchased from the United States, languished in prison. After several days, with the provincial army commanders begging for air support, it ceased being important whether they were still loyal in their hearts to the shah. President Bani-Sadr called the pilots to service. Whisked from prison cells to the cockpits of their fighter planes, they quickly slowed the Iraqi advance.

During the first weeks of war, normal life ground to a halt. Government offices and private companies closed early, so that people could rush home to take shelter. Restaurants and cinemas shut down, and after dark, Tehran's wide streets yawned empty and silent. Since no one knew when the Iraqi planes would come, raining their bombs down on the city, people grew wary of stepping outside. Most began carrying small radios, so they wouldn't miss air-raid alerts when they darted out to pick up groceries. Soon shops ran short of basic goods like sugar, flour, and detergent, and the government started a rationing system. The lines snaked for blocks, and sometimes it could take an entire day just to buy a bag of flour. Prices skyrocketed, and goods on the free market were impossibly expensive. My mother would sometimes call in the morning to see what I needed in the house. I was still going to work and didn't have the time, between Negar and the office, to wait in those long lines.

Gradually, the lines and shortages became ordinary, and we forgot the days when you could slip down to the *baghali*, the corner shop, and buy whatever you needed in five minutes. Restaurants slowly began opening again in the evenings, and throwing a birthday party stopped seeming inappropriate. Elderly couples resumed their afternoon strolls. We adapted to being at war, just as we had adapted to the chaos and upheaval of revolution. How amazing and yet tragic it is, I thought, the human instinct for survival.

The war effectively stanched popular discontent with the revolution. The suffocating political repression of the early revolution had by no means abated; we still woke up to morning newspapers filled with long lists of the executed, all the former regime's officials and the so-called counterrevolutionaries who had been shot or hung. I would turn the pages, sometimes filled with macabre photos of gallows and dead bodies, and shudder with revulsion at the secret show trials that preceded these executions. But there was no space, even at the margins, to express our anger. Even among ourselves, in our *dowrehs*—regular sessions where the like-minded gathered to discuss literature, the news, or whatever subjects struck their fancy—we refrained from airing our despair at the bloodletting.

I tried to be lighthearted, though our humor after the revolution had turned decidedly macabre. One day I picked up a newspaper during our *dowreh* and pulled out a calculator. "Given the number of people they are executing each month," I announced, "if we multiply the ratio by the population of Iran, the law of probability tells us that in seven years, ten months, and twenty-six days, it will be our turn." That's how quickly the death lists were published. This became a running joke among us, and we opened most of our meetings with a countdown: "Such-and-such number of days left!" How gruesome this sounds in retrospect. But what was the alternative? If we admitted to ourselves that the revolution had been betrayed, we would surely lose the war. We had to support the government, we thought, because it was the only one we had, and we were engaged in war with a brutal tyrant. Ayatollah Khomeini's revolution had not united Iranians, but the war, perforce, had imposed an ambivalent accord.

Saddam Hussein, butcher and despot, launched what he called the Qadisiya against Iran, ostensibly to redraw the borders and take control of Iran's oil-rich southern province. By invoking the Qadisiya, the seventh-century Arab-Muslim conquest of what was then Persia, Saddam sought to mythologize his war for territory and oil as a modern-day fight of Arab against Ajam. (*Ajam* is the Arabic word for a foreigner, specifically a Persian.) Ayatollah Khomeini, for his part, openly orated about his determination to spread his Shia revolution around the region. His revolutionaries claimed that Islam had no borders, and that nationalism, next to faith, was a cheap, worldly attitude. From Lebanon to Iraq, they saw fertile ground for a Shia Islamic uprising that would erase the artificial borders drawn by departing British colonizers. The ayatollah called the confrontation *jang-e tahmili*, the imposed war, and cast it as an ancient Shia struggle against despotism, painting Saddam as Yazid, the villain in Shia history who slaughtered Imam Hossein, the saint of Shiism, at the Battle of Karbala.

Apart from the two world wars, the century had witnessed little battlefield warfare so bloody. The Iran-Iraq War was the last of the twentieth century's wars of attrition, where two sovereign nations faced off, before the advent of military technology, and sent waves of young men onto battlefields by foot. Saddam had the advantage of access to the West's military cache, buying chemical agents from Western European firms and stores of weaponry from the United States. Iran, for its part, was the most populous nation in the region. It had human lives to spare.

The history of Iran's revolution and its war are inextricably intertwined. One followed the other so swiftly that the revolution forged its ideology and symbolism in the prosecution of war. To inspire the legions of young men to volunteer for the front with promises of a shortcut to heaven, a cult of martyrdom emerged that gloried human sacrifice in the name of Islam. Every night, the television showed footage of the young recruits, wearing red bandannas and their keys to heaven around their necks, boarding buses for the Iraqi battlefields. Many were barely in their teens, and they carried small Korans, along with portraits of Ayatollah Khomeini and Imam Ali, the first Shia imam. Some packed their funeral shrouds. The Iraqi army had laid mines across much of its border, and the Iranian command used these young recruits as human minesweepers, sending them across the plains in wave after wave, to clear the battlefield for the soldiers to the rear.

The defense of homeland became *defa-e moqaddas,* the sacred defense. Battlefield operations carried names such as Allaho Akbar and Imam Mahdi; bases were named Karbala and Qods. The Revolutionary Guards told us that the West had refused them even barbed wire and assault rifles. Ayatollah Khomeini said God had commanded the war.

Freshly wounded by a violent revolution, we put aside our grievances and betrayal. Those images marching across the television every night inflamed our nationalism. My heart cracked for our young men, setting out for Saddam's killing fields with their shoddy weapons, no match for a dictator armed with the latest from the West's arms boutiques. The young soldiers fought so well, we all thought, defending us brilliantly.

How to begin describing the gradual infusion of martyrdom into our lives? How to convey the slow process by which everything— public space, rituals, résumés, newspapers, television—became dominated by death, mourning, and grief? At the time, it didn't feel alien or excessive, this engorged enthusiasm for martyrdom and the aesthetic of death.

I continued my work at the ministry, but I had been assigned to a new position as "specialist" in the Guardianship Office of Minors and the Mentally Ill, which was part of the public prosecutor's office in Tehran. We assigned legal guardians to the mentally incapacitated and to children without fathers or paternal grandfathers. Mothers came into my office daily to inquire about their children's legal guardianship. At the start of the day, the office reverberated with the sounds of screaming and hollering children, followed, in midafternoon, by a complete silence.

My new office sat directly opposite a courtyard at the ministry where mass funerals for the war dead were convened. None of my relatives had gone to the front, but I experienced a hundred painful funerals just by virtue of where my office was located. I remember the first one vividly.

It began with the loudspeakers playing the soulful intonations of the prayer of mourning. About twenty coffins draped in the Iranian flag were carried into the courtyard and converged on by keening relatives. The soldiers were so young that many of their elderly grandparents were present, hobbling to keep up. The loudspeakers then blared the funeral march, and the procession began. I hid my face, turning it to the wall so the tears could stream down without my secretary seeing. I didn't want her to think I was so weak, crying at the funeral of strangers. This horrible scene became an almost daily occurrence. Eventually I couldn't take it anymore and shut the windows, so at least those piercing sobs would be muffled by the glass. I sweated through the summer, preferring to bear the heat in my head scarf and Islamic uniform, rather than hear the wails wafting up from below.

On April 30, 1982, a few hours before the inky, sweltering night lightened, about forty thousand young men armed with deep faith and rusted Kalashnikovs crossed the Arvand River and set out across the minefields. At night, the charred, decapitated tops of the palm trees and the blackened, torched dirt gave the landscape an almost lunar feel. The capturing of Khorramshahr, a strategic port city along the southern part of the waterway dividing Iran and Iraq, had been a blow to the Iranian defense, the only major Iranian city fallen to Saddam. That night, Iran's commanders whispered *Ali ibn Abi Taleb* (the password of Operation Beit ol-Moqaddas), drove their men into the heart of two fully armored Iraqi battalions, and persevered to wrest it back.

In the operation's first and second phases, waves of Iranian soldiers pushed around the city's environs, under heavy air raids, and liberated miles; in the third push (password *Mohammed, the Messenger of God*), they built a bridge across the river and circled the main road around the city for the final assault. On May 24, they marched triumphantly through the city, taking twelve thousand Iraqis prisoner. So much blood was let in Khorramshahr that Ayatollah Khomeini dubbed it "Khooninshahr," the city of blood. And when his soldiers claimed victory, he said, "God freed Khorramshahr."

We were following these events breathlessly, and rejoiced. Khorramshahr had been liberated! The war could finally end. Until the Revolutionary Guards reclaimed the city, we had all been in agreement that Iran should continue fighting, even though by that point at least one hundred thousand of our young soldiers had been killed. But the Battle of Khorramshahr was a political and military turning point; we regained our territory, and Saddam's better-armed forces saw that they were no match for a war command willing to prosecute with human waves. We assumed, with great relief, that the war would end.

Indeed, the next month, Saddam himself offered a truce. But at that time the radicals had not yet consolidated the revolution, and Tehran was a battlefield between the Mojahedin-e Khalgh Organization (MKO) and Ayatollah Khomeini's nascent regime. The MKO had emerged in the sixties, taking its inspiration from the guerrilla movements of Cuba and South America. Its leaders saw in Iran a similar semifeudal system ripe for class upheaval, but worried that young Iranians' vast potential for mobilization would be lost if they directed the struggle along secular Communist or socialist lines. The nascent political factions of the time had already set themselves apart from one another on the basis of theoretical and, in the eyes of the MKO, immaterial distinctions. In an Iranian context, they believed, aligning oneself as a Maoist versus a Leninist, or a Marxist versus a Trotskyist, was simply an intellectual indulgence, preoccupying young people with the unique strains of their discontent, rather than its goal: the overthrow of the Pahlavi monarchy through armed struggle.

To counter such fragmentation, the MKO's leaders fashioned a socialist, militant reading of Islam that resonated particularly with the educated middle class, who were cultured enough to interpret religion moderately but steeped enough in Iranian tradition to respond to the grassroots power of its call. In the late sixties and early seventies, the MKO's appeal was propelled by the work of the leading sociologist-intellectual of the day, a Sorbonne-educated sociologist by the name of Ali Shariati. It was an age when sociologists could be both heroes and militants, and Shariati, beloved by millions, was both. Though he is little known in the West, it is hard to overstate his role in the slow radicalization of Iranian youth in that era. Shariati recast the dominant narrative of Shiism—the struggle of the martyr in his fight against injustice—to emphasize resistance rather than defeat. His lectures masterfully invoked Iranians' discomfort with the free-fall Westernization of the shah and made modern heroes out of the seventh-century Shia figures of Imam Ali and the prophet Mohammed's daughter Fatemeh.

Ever utopian, Shariati promised Iranians that Islam would solve their modern-day problems, that if they reacquainted themselves with their "real" tradition (rather than its passivist legacy), if, in his words, they "re-became themselves," the way out of their modern problems would reveal itself. The Islamist utopian made Iranian society fertile ground for the rise of the MKO, and it is difficult to illustrate the group's social following without mentioning Shariati, a name that was on everyone's lips for years, when few knew or thought of Ayatollah Khomeini. It was Shariati who inspired masses of Iranians to support militant Islam over secular leftism, and the MKO flag always flew along with those of other groups at the head of the great marches. Though much of the history of the revolution remains contested, some believe that it was the MKO that propelled its victory.

But when Ayatollah Khomeini took power in 1979, his revolutionary government kept the MKO at arm's length, and in 1981 the group relaunched its armed struggle against the new leadership. Uprisings in Tehran and around the country were brutally put down, and the government moved to wipe its MKO opposition out entirely, sending its leaders underground and into exile, and arresting anyone with suspected sympathies. Though the MKO's allies and sympathizers would fall away in the years to come, it managed for a time to assassinate' officials and bomb government buildings in Tehran with some regularity.

The attacks held Tehran in a state of suspended semianarchy. The more radical in the ayatollah's court convinced him that we should push forward, straight to Baghdad, to unseat Saddam. If Iran could conquer ancient Mesopotamia, the land between the two rivers, what a regional powerhouse it would become, they argued. Obviously, this was delusional. Iran could never have pulled this off, and neither would the world—or at least Saddam's Western backers—have permitted it. But push for Mesopotamia we did, and Khorramshahr, instead of being the battle that ended our suffering, became the muse for the Islamic Republic's romance with its war.

*B*ack in Tehran, I cocked my head sideways, scanning the books on our bookshelf, plucking out the politically objectionable titles, and tossing them into a cardboard box. I lugged the box into the backyard. Negar watched me from behind the sliding glass door, mystified, as I made little pyramids around the periphery of the yard and then set them alight. A pile of Marx. A pile of Lenin. Sometimes I wondered whether she would retain memories of these strange times, when the adults used words like "execution" and "arrest" regularly in the kitchen, when her mother crouched in the backyard making bonfires out of books. I had started keeping a file of clippings from the newspapers to present to her later, when she would be old enough to demand explanations and my own memories, hopefully, would have faded. A thin whorl of smoke rose from each pile, as if I were performing some esoteric ritual. When the last volume collapsed into a small heap of ash, soot covered the shrubs and lilies in the garden, and charred pages blew around, like paper leaves.

Earlier that week, the newspapers had begun announcing the firing-squad executions of those suspected of sympathizing with leftist groups deemed counterrevolutionary. Ever since the shah had left and Ayatollah Khomeini had returned, the various political factions had split and metastasized, and then fought each other over the revolution's direction; to entrench their control, the circle around the ayatollah had begun hunting down members and suspected sympathizers of the groups they sought to sideline. Each current published its own magazines and books, espousing its particular definition of revolution, and many Iranians bought them, amassing small libraries of political texts that cataloged the different strains of the revolution. But when the purges began, being caught in possession of a targeted group's literature was considered a crime, an act of opposition to the regime. Book owners, and even the families of book owners, could be sentenced to years in prison.

It was a tense time, and everyone felt uncomfortable in their own skin. Javad invited his little brother Fuad, the youngest in the family, to come and stay with us for a time. Fuad was a sweet seventeen-year-old, enchanted with the revolution's idealism. Like many young people at the time, he was attracted to the Mojahedin-e Khalgh, impressed by their insistence that the revolutionary vision of freedom and independence had yet to be reached, and started selling the group's booklets at his school. In those days young people were easily attracted to ideology; "you are such a liberal" was the ugliest insult of the day. If you were a liberal, it meant you were wary of ideology, that you were either lazy and couldn't be bothered to have beliefs or were a coward and refused to stand behind them.

The regime and the MKO confronted each other daily at the time, and there were frequent crackdowns on the group's leadership, which eventually broadened to include junior sympathizers like Fuad. The previous week a number of his friends had been arrested. Afraid of being followed and putting his elderly parents at risk, he started spending the night at our house instead. It was Ramadan (pronounced *Ramazan* in Persian) then, the holy month of fasting, and he would show up at eleven each night and fall asleep in our spare room. One of the first couple of nights he stayed over, I gently shook him awake before dawn. I'd made him a small wrap of *lavash* and dates, just a simple presunrise meal that fasters traditionally took so they could make it through the day until *iftar*, the breaking of the fast. Fuad blinked sleepily through his long lashes and shook his head. "Just have a few bites," I said, "you'll need the energy." "No," he said in a groggy whisper, "I want to feel hungry like poor people do." I switched off the light, pulled the duvet over his slim, still-adolescent shoulders, and let him go back to sleep.

One afternoon, Fuad bounded into the house and asked if he

could borrow my aged typewriter. He didn't say what he needed it for, but I didn't think to question him. It was just a typewriter, after all. When Javad came home that night and noticed the typewriter missing, he was furious. "What were you thinking?" he snapped at me. "You know we're never going to get it back." Javad got frightened more easily than I did. He didn't actually say it—in those days, we still tried to hide our terror—but he was worried about where that typewriter could end up, and whether it could be traced back to us. "Well, he's your *brother*," I said. "It's not like I could say no to him. Besides, I wasn't using it anyway."

Javad was right, of course. The typewriter was never returned. But Javad and I found more to fight about. Fuad, distracted with his utopian visions of a purer, more just Islamic revolution, often left things lying around. As I was packing my bag one morning for work, I noticed an MKO book about Imam Hossein on our bookcase. I started leafing through it; for the literature of an organization that later became a cult, it was rather interesting. That night Fuad and I were discussing the book in the kitchen when Javad came home. He picked it up and realized it was MKO material.

"Do you think, Fuad *jan*," he asked sharply, "that it was responsible to leave this on the shelf? Why did you leave it here?"

"But I've already burned all the other political books," I interrupted. "Just one isn't that important." I felt protective of Fuad, this young man who called his friends "brother" and wasn't so knocked out and full of despair at the course of the revolution to forsake it, and retreat inside as we had.

"Please." Fuad held a hand up, as though to stop me from defending him. "Javad is right—we shouldn't have this book in the house. But," he promised with a shining, determined look, "in two months this book will be promoted on television. You'll see." The MKO, in the manner of all political groups struggling to draw sympathizers, had assured their followers that the regime would fall fast.

The next day, Fuad walked to the university, as usual. His empty stomach growling, he passed the spice vendors' stalls, the burlap sacks filled to the brim with sunny yellow lentils, dusty dried limes, and slivered almonds. Perhaps in the wheeze of the buses and the clink-clank of the construction sites, he didn't hear the footsteps too close behind him. "Fuad!" He spun around when his name was called, and before he realized what was happening, his arms were roughly tied behind his back and he was thrust toward a waiting car.

For three nights, we heard nothing. I tried to believe he was hiding out with his MKO friends, holed up somewhere drinking tea and imagining the revolution's rescue. On the fourth day, his mother was informed that he had been arrested. Frantic, she began phoning everyone she could think of, and eventually managed to contact the prime minister. "I can only mediate," he told her, "if your son recants his views and cooperates with the regime."

Explain that to a teenage boy swept up in the euphoria of a revolution, convinced of his innocence. And he was innocent. What had he done? At the age of seventeen, for the crime of selling newspapers, Fuad was sentenced to twenty years in prison. While in prison, Fuad refused to cooperate with the prison authorities. In the context of prison, a bland word like "cooperation" usually means naming friends (who can then be dragged into similar interrogation chambers, to then name *their* friends), begging pardon, renouncing all political affiliations, surrendering to the will of God. In prison, cooperation is not requested; it is induced. Once they beat him so badly that they broke his jaw. And then they called his mother and demanded money to have it reset. Another time, they broke his arm. Again, the call came: Fuad's broken arm is dangling at his side, they said. If you want it treated, send cash.

Javad's father was killed in a car accident later that year, and the family requested a leave from the prison for Fuad to participate in the funeral. Their uncle signed papers at the prison, guaranteeing his return, and Fuad came out for a one-night bereavement furlough. When he showed up at the house with his uncle, at first I didn't recognize him. Could that be Fuad? That pale, shrinking boy with the hesitant gaze? To this day, I regret the first words out of my mouth when I saw him. "Fuad, be a man today," I said. I meant that he should be strong for his nearly hysterical mother and check his own grief for his father. But he misunderstood. He thought I was criticizing him for not being tough enough in prison, during interrogation.

"I *am* a real man, and I've proven it," he said, in a high voice that turned heads. The relatives began noticing his arrival and slowly surrounded him. About half an hour later, he said he wanted to escape from prison. All the heads around him shook at once, as though on cue. No! A terrible idea. . . . What about your uncle, who guaranteed you. . . . You'll be caught, and then what! A torrent of dissent.

I beckoned Javad across the room and whispered to him urgently. "Why not? Why don't you all let the boy escape?"

"If he escapes, he'll most likely go straight to the MKO," Javad said. "And then he will certainly be killed. I know, I dread him going back too. But at least in there, he's alive." When Fuad saw that the relatives wouldn't budge, he fell silent and refused to utter another word the rest of the night. After dinner, when he had to use the restroom, a relative followed him to the door and ordered him to keep it unlocked. They worried he might flee from out the window. At the end of the night, he got in the car with his uncle, stared straight ahead, and let himself be driven back to prison.

CHAPTER FIVE

War of the Cities

FOR A FULL TWO YEARS NOW, THE REGIME HAD MADE THE head scarf compulsory for women, but I still forgot. Usually, in the last few seconds before I flew out the door, I'd make a quick survey of the living room, sensing that I was missing something. Keys? Shopping list? Once I walked all the way down the block and noticed the whole street—from our old neighbor strolling with his cane to the kids playing on their stoop—staring at me. I couldn't imagine why, especially since my step was light and I felt more comfortable than most days. "*Khanum* Ebadi," one of the neighbors eventually cried out, "you've forgotten your *hejab!*" I ran all the way home and tied one of the cotton scarves around my head.

"Just think of it," I told one of my girlfriends on the phone that night. "If a policeman had seen me, I would've been arrested."

"That's nothing," she said. "Last week, I drove off without remembering mine. I was in traffic already, stopped at an intersection, when I saw that all the people crossing the street were giving me surprised looks. What could I do? I was already in the car. So I yanked my skirt all the way up, and pulled it over my hair."

Eventually, I hung a veil on a tack in the hallway, to remind me.

In those times, just as today, a sizable number of Iranian women would have gone bareheaded, if given the freedom to choose. But the war years called upon us to endure, not reflect. Women's anger with the imposed *hejab* (a symbol of their broader lack of rights) had not yet moved to the forefront of their consciousness. Similarly, political discontent with the new regime—its censorship, its brutal extermination of its opponents, its radical decision to extend the war—was still a private dismay, rather than the dominant public mood.

In 1983, our second daughter, Nargess, was born. Javad and I had agreed that if the baby was a boy, he would pick the name, but that if we had a daughter I would choose. I named her after a flower that blooms in winter, the *nargess*. When I went into labor, my mother took Negar, then three, to her house, promising that we would return with a playmate for her. I had consulted several books of child psychology on how best to introduce a new baby to a young toddler. I bought Negar new clothes, toys, chocolates, all of her favorite

This photograph with my daughters was taken for our joint passport.

things, as gifts from her new sister. I made sure to lay Nargess down in her crib, for the moment the nanny brought Negar over from my mother's. Javad stood poised near the door, waiting to capture the moment when Negar rushed into my arms. She couldn't stand being apart from me, and it had been two days, our longest separation.

I pulled the door open with a bright smile. Javad changed positions, with his camera. Negar sailed right past me, without even a glance. Crossing her little arms over her chest, she marched into the living room and sat silently on the couch. I wasn't prepared for how the anger of my three-year-old girl would affect me. I was racked with guilt for making her suffer.

Their sibling rivalry and childhood antics animated my life at a time when my depressing work ended and the depression of not working began. A year after Nargess was born, I became eligible for retirement from the ministry. Civil servants could retire after fifteen years of service, with pension. Exactly one day after my fifteen years, I put in my retirement request, which of course was swiftly accepted by the ministry, only too glad to rid itself of that great nuisance, the female employee.

The year I retired was a turning point for me, and for my women friends from the university who had started their careers around the same time. Enough time had passed that it was clear the system was not going to change in any substantive way. Its ideology was fixed, and for the time being, so was its tolerance threshold for women in government. It was a time when you had to weigh your ambitions, sensibilities, and ethics, and decide how you were going to deal with the new regime. My indignation ran too deep and my personality was too rebellious for me to do anything but vent my scorn at every opportunity. Retirement was the only choice that made any sense. It never occurred to me to think of the career consequences, for in my mind the regime had already killed our careers. I never thought that one day the revolutionary regime might mellow, and that perhaps there would be a judiciary career for me if I hushed myself in the present. My friend Maryam, the passionate fellow judge from my university days, was more calculating. She took on the mantle of clerkship as though there were no greater honor than demotion. Our friendship suffered, and the last afternoon we ever met for tea, when I told her I was retiring, we fought acrimoniously. Her saccharine new attitudes and—in my view—turncoat behavior disappointed me deeply, and I finally blurted out my private thoughts.

"Maryam, why did you even become a judge in the first place?" I asked. "I can't believe you're willing to abandon your principles like this."

"You don't know this regime," she retorted. "Keep on running your mouth if you wish, and just see how they'll come for you. You'll get harassed, you'll lose your job."

"You mean this jewel of a job, this clerkship? This job you love so much that you've forgotten who you are and you've abandoned your old friends?"

She stared at me in shock. Even among friends, it was almost taboo in Iranian culture to invoke reality so harshly.

I went on to say many things in anger that sealed the ruin of our friendship, but at that point she had stopped socializing with me in public anyway (since being seen with a critic like me could taint her reputation), so I didn't feel there was that much to lose. I told her she wanted power for power's sake and was willing to trample on any-thing—her friends, her values—to get there. I told her that even if she was one day promoted to some exalted position, it would be an empty victory, for seniority in an unpopular system was more damn-ing than being a sidelined nobody. That pretty much ended things for Maryam and me. In the years to come, we periodically attended the same conferences. She was usually the cheery woman in a chador trilling on about how Islamic law had emancipated Iranian women. We did not greet each other when we passed in the hallways.

Our old friend Sara, the scholar among us who'd married the law professor, did not make a point of criticizing the new laws as I did, but she also did not espouse them in the manner of Maryam. She had been hired by the Foreign Ministry to work on international trade law shortly before the revolution, and because she was a low-profile researcher, the ministry kept her on, though several years passed before she received a long overdue promotion. In that time, Sara managed to avoid selling out her beliefs. She never pretended to support the new regime, and by and large she kept her opinions about its practices outside the narrow realm of trade law very private. In later years, she represented the Islamic Republic at international trade conferences, but she spoke only about her area of expertise and refused to address questions about women's legal status, even when they were posed to her.

The Foreign Ministry knew that Sara was no devoted believer, but her superiors found her expertise useful, and the field was specialized enough that she could carry forth without being called on to legitimize what she opposed. For me, Sara illustrated the slim, fortunate strata of professional Iranians whose fields were relatively apolitical and permitted them to work and prosper in their limited realms. Of course, that did not mean it was easy for her. I'm certain that along the way she watched inferior colleagues promoted past her, and knew she would never ascend to her full potential. She was bright enough to have become a finance minister, but she was female, too unrevolutionary, and too unrelated to the political elite to ascend to such heights. Yet she managed to keep working, to illustrate that, yes, it is suffocating to work in the Islamic Republic, but it is not always necessary to be a mouthpiece in order to have a career.

Today, when I try to tell stories of the mid-eighties or remember what my life was like in those years when my girls were small and the war raged on, the only images that come to mind are a disjointed series of living room memories. Our family struggled in those years and spent most of our days indoors, at home. I had retired, and Javad's firm was shut down on the grounds that it had been infiltrated by Communists. There were long stretches when we had little income. Inflation was high, and with two children, our expenses were also high. To afford necessities such as diapers and powdered milk for the kids, we slashed our spending habits and cut out luxuries like the occasional restaurant meal. Both girls loved eating out, and they would clamor in the evenings for something more special than our usual dinner in the kitchen. So I moved our dining table to a different corner of the apartment, spread out a fresh tablecloth, and inaugurated "Shirin's Restaurant." "Welcome, ladies," I would say, and I pretended to take their orders as they sidled up to our make-believe café. I hoped they were learning to create opportunities out of what they had to work with. I hoped they were learning the pleasure of delayed gratification.

The backdrop to those quiet years in the living room was ugly. In 1984, Saddam Hussein unleashed chemical weapons on the Iranian army for the first time. He started out by using sarin, an utterly odorless nerve gas that kills a few minutes after inhalation. Once it became clear that Saddam would use what Winston Churchill had called "that hellish poison" as a routine weapon, the Iranian command armed its young soldiers with syringes of atropine, an antidote to nerve gas, but in the sweltering conditions most still stood no chance. There was not enough chemical gear to go around, and in the unbearable desert heat the few soldiers equipped with masks either did not wear them or could not seal them tightly enough around their beards. They were fighting a war God had commanded, after all, and a proper Muslim man wears a beard, especially when packed for heaven. Often the syringes malfunctioned or the atropine lost its potency in the heat. Survivors reported gruesome accounts of battlefields strewn with syringes among the bodies, the soldiers having tried to inject themselves in the precious minutes between the first lethal inhalation and death.

Saddam dispensed of nerve gas quickly and switched to what became his favorite chemical weapon, the blister agent known as mustard gas. Unlike nerve gas, mustard carries a distinct scent—oddly enough, of garlic—but it has no antidote and kills with excruciating slowness. Shortly after the soldiers on the front caught its first whiff, their vision blurred and they began coughing uncontrollably, often vomiting at the same time. As the hours crept by, their skin began to blister, darkening first to a deep purple. Next, whole patches of skin fell off, and their armpits and groins turned black with lesions. Those who survived were hospitalized for a few days to a few weeks, depending on the severity of their exposure. If they regained functionality, they were sent back to the front.

By and large, the world watched mutely. U.N. missions investigated and found evidence of Iraq's use of chemical weapons, but no coalition of the willing emerged to condemn the Iraqi dictator, let alone to try to stop him. The United States, seeking to contain and weaken the revolutionary regime it deemed hostile to its interests in the region, even strengthened Iraq's hand. Former military officials in Washington later confirmed what the Iranian command had believed all along—that the Reagan administration provided Iraq with satellite images of Iranian troop deployment. In later years it also emerged that a covert American program had extended far more serious battle-planning assistance than that, at a time when U.S. intelligence agencies knew that Iraq was using chemical weapons in most major operations. With international public opinion silent, the world's greatest superpower assisting Saddam Hussein, and the clerical regime in Tehran bent on prolonging their "sacred defense," we soon realized the end was nowhere near. It was at about this time that the flight of Iranians out of the country began in earnest.

After the revolution, a wave of Iranians had fled the country; those who'd opposed the revolution and those who'd feared for their lives because of their ties to the regime had flown to Europe or the United States and started new lives in the West. But once it became clear that the war would drag on, that Saddam would use chemical poisons and get away with it, a wide stratum of people started to leave, especially those with sons, who feared they would be drafted and killed at the front. Each day the numbers swelled. Some managed to obtain visas and boarded planes at Mehrabad Airport, safety and dignity intact. Hundreds of thousands of others, desperate to get out at any cost, paid bandits to smuggle them overland through Turkey or Pakistan. The smugglers reaped vast profits, herding Iranians in the dead of night through the gorges and desert passes of the country's borders; it was risky to leave this way, but it was even riskier to stay, their thinking went.

Those who left mostly scattered themselves across Europe and North America, with pockets collecting first in Los Angeles and European capitals like Paris and London. Later emigrants sought refuge in Scandinavia, and Canada's relatively open borders drew Iranians to Vancouver and Toronto. From working class to wealthy, they left in droves, filling the leather markets of Florence, dealing cocaine in the streets of Tokyo, running vast rug empires in Manhattan. Educated professionals saturated Silicon Valley and the East Coast of the United States with doctors, engineers, and bankers, while socialites held court in Kensington and Beverly Hills. The estimates are rough, but approximately four to five million Iranians left over two decades, among them the country's brightest. To this day, Iran sustains one of the most serious brain drains in the world; those of us who stayed have watched our young people fan out across the world, animating the societies and economies of nations other than our own.

Emigration does not figure dramatically in the story of modern Iran, in the sense that its images, unlike those of war and the revolution, are not cinematic shots of limb-strewn battlefields or three-million-person marches of extended fists. But if you ask most Iranians what *keeneh*, what grievance, they nurture most bitterly against the Islamic Republic, it is the tearing apart of their families. Memories of war fade, and very few people have the energy to sustain intellectual distress over the course of a lifetime, but the absence of loved ones—the near-permanent separation of sister from sister, mother from daughter—is a pain that time does not blunt. Shall I count for you the number of families I know who once upon a time all lived in the same city and are now dispersed across the globe, each child in a different Western city, the parents in Iran? In the eyes of many, the Islamic Republic is to blame for this; had the revolutionaries tempered their wild radicalism, had they not replaced the shah with a regime that prompted mass flight, their families would still be whole.

One by one, my dearest friends deserted. They packed up their belongings, said their good-byes, and, in my eyes, turned their backs on Iran. Each time I wearily picked up a pen to cross out yet another name in my address book, my disappointment crushed me. I felt as though I were living in an abandoned house that was decaying by the day, in the company of ghosts.

In the beginning, I fought them. Each and every one of them, when they declared their intent to leave, faced my perhaps unfair flood of dissuasion and protest. I knew that the decision to leave was deeply personal. And, true, I didn't have sons. But all the same, as an ethical and political stand, I didn't believe in leaving Iran.

One of my cousins called the week he was leaving for Germany and asked me to drop by. As he wandered around his apartment packing, he kept repeating that he was leaving "for the children." I finally exploded. "Look around you! Don't you see a nation full of Iranians around you, all of them with children? Their children are studying here. What's your problem? Just stay and let the kids go to school here."

"There's no future for them here. I need to take them somewhere where they have a future."

"What about the future of all the kids who will stay? Does staying mean that they have no future?"

"If your kids were older, Shirin *jan*, you would leave too."

"No, I would never abandon Iran," I retorted. "If my kids had to leave, I would send them. Each generation needs to stay in the place it was raised. If you and I leave Iran, what are we going to do? Here we're somebody. We're accomplished, and have worked to reach a certain position in this society. Our friends, like us, are bright and educated. If we go abroad, do you think we'll be accepted—with our foreign degrees and foreign accents—with open arms? Our kids are young, and they'll absorb the culture of their new world. And after some time passes, we'll lose them too."

He looked unconvinced. I tried another approach.

"Look, a girl who has grown up abroad from the age of seven will likely marry a foreigner. Naturally, she'll adapt to his culture, and distance will slowly creep between us. One day we'll wake up and realize we can never exist in each other's worlds—her in ours, and us in hers—in the same way again. We should think about this, anticipate such a day from right now, and keep our children here. Later on, in the final stage of their studies, they can go abroad for a time. But they'll have been formed here. Like us, they'll adapt to whatever painful reality lies in store, and this place will be lodged in their hearts. They'll come back."

A long silence followed the conclusion of my speech. My cousin exhaled a long sigh, looked away, and kept packing. "Take whatever you need," he told me, gesturing at the housewares strewn about. And though I needed some of his things, I refused to touch anything and left. I didn't want the platter or end table of someone who had left me, and his country, behind.

There were many more such living room dramas to come. A friend of mine decided to put the innards of her house on sale, and called me over one day to keep her company. I found her whirling about herself in the living room, sticking little price tags on everything in sight. I was hoping we would have tea together and talk first, but like most of the nearly departed she busied her way through the final days, retreating from conversation in a forest of boxes and packing tape. I trailed her around the living room, angrily pulling off each sticker she affixed. We faced off, both of us with fingers covered in sticky white price tags. Just then, the ring of the doorbell interrupted us. It was only three-thirty, half an hour before the sale was meant to start.

A large woman entered and began inspecting candlesticks and picture frames with beady eyes, as though my friend's living room, where her children had taken their first steps, was a stall in the bazaar. I was incensed. I had half an hour to work on my friend, to persuade her to change her mind, and now this bargain vulture was stealing my time. I grabbed her arm and led her outside. Stand there until it's four o'clock, I said, and slammed the door.

"Please," I begged my friend inside. "Stop this madness. What are you doing? *This is our country!*"

But at four o'clock, the sale began. None of my sentimental appeals prompted my friends or relatives to reconsider. Probably it did not seem worth it, to surrender daily happiness and future ambition to the distant goal of rehabilitating the country. Eventually my address book filled with crossed-out numbers; I could tear out certain pages entirely. In a way, when I look back across years filled with pain and difficulty, I see this as the bottom moment. I had lost my beloved profession. I had lost my country. And I had lost my friends.

I refused to write letters to those who had left. I tried a couple of times, but the pen felt like a dead weight in my hands, and the idea of actually filling those pages made me despair. It reminded me that I had lost those I loved, that they were now absent from my life. They would call on the phone and say, "Shirin *jan*, just a note, don't you know how happy a short note from you would make us?" But I couldn't. Some of my friends were hurt, but over time I hope they saw that my stubbornness stemmed from an excess of devotion, rather than its lack.

When someone leaves Iran, it's as though that person has died to me. We're friends so long as we share the same world, for as long as the same hopes illuminate our lives, the same anxieties keep us awake at night. Years later, when my friends traveled back to Iran for short visits, I saw how right I had been. We still spoke Farsi, the same blood still ran through our veins, but they were living on a different planet than I was. You could find the words we exchanged in the same Persian dictionary, but it was as though we spoke different languages. In reality, I had lost my friends. Effectively, *my* friends—the ones who once shopped at the same produce stands and stared in shock at the same newspaper headlines—were dead. You wouldn't correspond with a dead person, would you? In the same way it would never occur to me to write letters to the dead (a nonsensical, hurtful task, wouldn't you agree?), it never occurs to me to write to my friends who have left Iran. It's because I love them so dearly, not because I have forgotten them. I love them so much that picking up a pen and composing the opening paragraph of a letter hurts me. In the absence of correspondence, the distance and stark contrast in our lives remains obscured.

One year, in the middle of the war, Javad and I decided to take the family on a trip to India. After we arrived, Saddam announced that he would officially begin targeting commercial airliners. We fretted about the flight back the whole time we were there, and when the plane entered Iranian airspace, all the passengers bent their heads and began whispering their prayers, as though it were a hajj, or pilgrimage, flight to Mecca. As we were driving home from Mehrabad Airport, tenser than when we had left, Javad decided we should avoid airplanes until the war ended.

After that trip, time passed in drips. The year 1988 marked a new phase in the war, the War of the Cities. Iraqi air strikes, until then intermittent and confined to strategic areas along the border front, became a daily occurrence in Tehran and other cities. The roar of Iraqi fighter planes became the background noise to our lives, and some days as many as twenty missiles would hit the city. It was the year the war came into our neighborhoods, turned our nights inside out.

The Iraqi military declared that it was not bombing cities to kill civilians but, rather, to induce them to press the government to accept a cease-fire. To that purported end, it used satellite imagery of Tehran to select neighborhoods for pinpoint strikes, and announced the evening's target on the morning news, so that residents would have time to clear out. Those with means or a place to stay fled their homes; others spent the night sleepless in their beds. Either the Iraqi command was incapable of smart bombing or was waging psycho-logical warfare, because only rarely did the missiles hit their desig-nated targets. The day the announcer said, "Tonight we are hitting Yusefabad," our neighborhood, I phoned my parents and said we should find someplace else to sleep that night. My father refused, implacable. "Whatever is meant to happen will happen," he said. So we all slept over at my parents' place, figuring if we were meant to perish, we might as well perish together. We shared a potentially last supper of lamb stewed with dried limes and yellow lentils, sipped tea while staring distractedly at the television, and filed off to bed. Nothing happened in the end, and we kissed each other's haggard faces at breakfast, feeling awkwardly relieved that it had not been our turn, knowing it almost certainly had been someone else's.

The assault on the cities spared all of our relatives, but a friend of Javad's was not so fortunate. He returned from work one evening to find that his house, his wife, and their two daughters had all been incinerated in a missile strike during his commute. With his whole life obliterated, he nearly went mad.

Horrific stories like this one drove Iranians to leave Tehran. Those who could afford to leave their jobs relocated to the prov-inces. The forward-looking wealthy took up permanent residence in hotels, the once stately Hiltons and Hyatts whose towers were not targeted, and could have sustained strikes even if they were. Renamed and state-operated, the hotels swarmed with guest residents paying three to four times the normal rates.

One night I wandered around the lobby of the former Sheraton, waiting to meet a visiting correspondent. (In 1987, after I had retired from work and before the war had ended, I had begun writing books so I could at least make scholarly contributions to the legal fields in which I could not work. Also, journalists would often seek me out as an expert on women's rights and other such legal matters.) Aghast, I paced back and forth between the restaurant and the coffee shop, ob-serving the coiffed, stylish young men and women dining with soft piano music in the background. They gracefully cut into steaks and poked spoons into crème caramel, while at the time half of what the rest of us in Tehran needed was not available at all and the other half required government coupons. The hotel lobby was like an isle of calm in the war-torn city, and it seemed as though the wealthy, with their freshly pressed clothes and tranquil expressions, experienced the war differently than the rest of us did.

The strikes Iranians were fleeing did not devastate the city block by block. If you drove through Tehran, you noticed only pockets of destruction. The Iraqi jets did not level the city, but they made us go about our daily lives in constant apprehension.

One morning in this period I went downtown to run some errands, and stood at a busy intersection, waiting for a taxi. After about fifteen minutes, sick from the fumes of the chugging buses, I started walking. I hadn't even reached the other end of the long block when a deafening boom resounded, the ground beneath me heaved, and I saw the pavement below me pass in a blur. The force threw me against the concrete side of a building, and I lay there slumped, blinking at the commotion around me. People were shouting and pointing toward the corner where I had been standing. I limped back, pushing my way through the crowd, past charred, smoking cars, and stared into a large crater, full of rubble and injured bodies.

That night, Javad insisted that Tehran was no longer safe and that we must leave the city. But my parents, elderly by that time and reluctant to move out of their house, refused to go. In the end, I agreed to take the kids and my sister to northern Iran, near the Caspian Sea, while Javad stayed in Tehran with my parents.

We rented a small house in one of the small town-cities of the north, and Negar rode her bike each day to a schoolhouse brimming with children from across the country, there to escape the war. Each night, she came home and bent over her homework until ten in the evening. Why, I wondered, did an eight-year-old have this much homework? I walked to school with her the next day, through the narrow streets and past unfinished cement fences that made this place look like a village compared to Tehran, to talk to her teacher.

"Each of my classes," explained the harried woman, "is three times over capacity. There aren't enough new books to go around, and I'm loading them up with lessons, just so they have something to do, so I can keep order."

A couple of months passed, and the government announced the end of the War of the Cities. We returned to Tehran.

On a summer evening in early July 1988, we turned on the television to see footage of bodies floating in the sea amid scattered airplane wreckage. Earlier that morning, a U.S. warship in the Persian Gulf had fired a heat-seeking missile at an Iranian civilian airliner, blowing it out of the sky. All 290 people on board perished, and it was their corpses Iranian television showed bobbing in the gulf's warm waters. President Ronald Reagan offered no convincing explanation of how the USS *Vincennes*, equipped with the most sophisticated radar gear in the navy's arsenal, had taken the bulky Iranian airbus for a sleek, supersonic fighter plane barely a third of its size. Few Iranians could believe this to be a mistake—we also noticed when the ship's captain received a medal for his performance—and the country's leaders stopped to reevaluate the war, imagining that the United States was finally going to take a side. America's intervention would not only help Saddam recover his lost ground but imperil Iran's revolution. They decided, nearly eight years and half a million lost lives later, to end the fighting and accept a Security Council cease-fire resolution. On July 18, the radio broadcast a historic statement from Ayatollah Khomeini. "I pledged to fight to the last drop of my blood," he said. "And though this decision is akin to drinking a chalice of poison, I submit myself to the will of God."

We all breathed in relief, hardly able to believe that the war, the backdrop of our lives, the only reality my daughters had ever known, had actually come to an end. Finally, we could stop focusing on whether or not there would be a missile strike tomorrow. We could stop planning our days around the lines for sugar. Would life become normal again? And what did "normal" even mean? The war had been fought primarily on Iranian territory. Our provincial farmland, our cities, our economy and industry had all been devastated. We had moved right from the stupor of revolution to embarking on the war, and now we had to recover, effectively, from both.

Six days later, the Mojahedin-e Khalgh dispatched seven thousand fighters from a base in Iraq to attack the western Iranian province of Kermanshah. In the late 1980s, the MKO had begun training its guerrillas in Iraq, and fighting alongside Saddam's army. By helping Saddam weaken the Iranian regime, their thinking went, they would advance their own aim of bringing down the government. Believing that the regime would be reeling from the cease-fire and vulnerable to a popular uprising, they decided it was finally time to march on Tehran. On the eve of the operation they termed Eternal Light, the MKO leader promised his troops that the Iranian masses would join their fight and lead them toward victory. "It will be like an avalanche, growing as it progresses. Eventually, the avalanche will tear Ayatollah Khomeini's web apart. You don't need to take anything with you. We will be like fish swimming in a sea of people."

How wrong they were, how tragically they miscalculated. The last thing Iranians wanted at that moment was more violence. And they would never forgive the MKO for taking up arms with Saddam's men, the troops who'd destroyed the lives of half a million young Iranian men, spraying whole battalions with nerve gas. The Revolutionary Guards swiftly crushed the MKO offensive, killing nearly eighteen hundred fighters and sending others fleeing back over the mountains to Iraq. In Tehran, family visits to MKO prisoners were suspended for three months. Why? we wondered nervously, thinking of Fuad.

*M*y mother-in-law received a phone call inquiring about her son Fuad on a cold morning in the fall of 1988. She was in her early seventies, and often strained to hear the voice on the other end of the line. She did not notice that the unidentified caller phrased his question in the past tense: "Did you have a son named Fuad?"

"Of course, yes, Fuad is my youngest."

"Then tell his father to report to Evin Prison tomorrow."

"His father passed away some years ago," she replied.

"Well, then tell his brother to come." And the line went dead.

The prison known as Evin is tucked away on the side of an expressway in northern Tehran that bears the same name. It is one of the few institutions in Iran whose reputation has passed unchanged from the shah's regime to the Islamic Republic. With its iron walls and low-slung architecture, the prison holds a grim reputation for having been the scene of thousands of executions since the revolution. The name Evin alone conjures images of basement interrogation chambers and long rows of dank, narrow solitary cells, and occupies perhaps the darkest corner of the Iranian imagination.

Javad and his uncle drove up the winding road that leads to the prison the next day, the peaks of the Alborz Mountains rising in the distance. It wasn't hard to find the right office: they just followed the path of ashen and sobbing relatives, back to where they were emerging from. "Here," said the prison marshal, handing Javad a bag. "These are your brother's possessions. He has been executed," he added, almost as an afterthought. "For one year you shall refrain from holding a funeral, or mourning his death in any public way. If after one year your conduct is deemed acceptable, we will reveal to you his place of burial."

The first thing Javad and his uncle did was search the contents of the bag. How could they be sure these were Fuad's things? With Evin crowded and overrun, how could the authorities properly account for each prisoner and his belongings? Perhaps they were simply running down a list of names and declaring people dead, when they were not. Javad pulled out a warm-up suit that he didn't recognize, a few pairs of undergarments that could have been anyone's. He rummaged at the bottom and his hand grasped a *tasbeeh*, a string of prayer beads, and then he knew that his little brother was dead. Fuad and his *tasbeeh* were inseparable; it was his favorite keepsake, dangling from his fingers even as he rushed to and from class.

From the prison, Javad called his sisters and asked them to prepare his mother for the news, and he asked me to drive over to her house immediately. As I quickly showered and dressed, a huge lump lodged in my throat, but I couldn't cry. I turned the key in the ignition, and when the notes of the haunting piano melody "Roozegar-e Ma" ("Our Times") echoed from the stereo, my tears began to fall. I cried all the way over, wiping my eyes with the tail end of my head scarf.

I cornered Javad in the kitchen at my mother-in-law's house, near the electric samovar that kept the tea hot, and asked him why Fuad had been executed. According to the prison officials, the MKO members killed in the Mersad attack (the name the government had given to the MKO attack) had notes pinned to their bodies, listing the names of their supporters in Evin. Fuad's name, apparently, had been on one of the lists. I laughed bitterly. A twenty-four-year-old boy, languishing in prison while serving a twenty-year sentence for selling newspapers, had somehow established contact with MKO fighters on the Iran-Iraq border? Even if he had, even if this flimsy allegation was somehow true, the prison guards would have been responsible, for permitting inmates to communicate with the outside. My mind reeled. How could someone summarily order the execution of an Iranian citizen already in prison for years, without a fresh conviction in a court of law?

What had he done? As a judge, I felt more acutely than anyone the great weight of a death sentence. An order of execution, the taking of a human life, is the ultimate decree of any justice system, and follows an exhaustive deliberation in keeping with the mortal gravity of the process. Fuad, this naive young boy, what had he done? His only crime was selling newspapers, a crime to which he had already surrendered his youth, serving seven years of a twenty-year sentence.

Executed! I could not absorb it. There is no law anymore, I thought to myself, and people's lives are so cheap.

That night, a mute fury settled in my stomach. When I think back and try to pinpoint the moment that changed me, the moment when my life took a different course, I see that it all began that night. My sister-in-law, a doctor, took one look at my face that evening and pulled out the cuff to check my blood pressure. As the little needle danced above the red mark, she told me I should go to the emergency room immediately. The next day, I began taking medication for high blood pressure, and for the rest of my life, I would start my day by swallowing a small handful of pills, prescribed to still my anxieties and keep my blood pressure down. Javad, for his part, went on medication for asthma, a previously light condition that turned quite severe and left him wheezing for air.

Fuad's death made me even more obstinate. We had been told not to discuss his death with anyone, so I talked about his execution night and day. In taxis, at the corner shop, in line for bread, I would approach perfect strangers and tell them about this sweet boy who was sentenced to twenty years in prison for selling newspapers, and then executed. No one looked at me strangely. They just listened, and sympathized. It never occurred to me that this might be dangerous, that there might be eavesdroppers registering who had disobeyed, who spoke about what they had been ordered to hide. There was just so much pain inside me that I needed to get it out. And perhaps if they hadn't told us not to, I wouldn't have felt the urge to shout it from the rooftops.

They told us not to mourn his death, but how could we not? Under the pretext of commemorating the anniversary of his father's death, we held a ceremony for Fuad and announced it in the newspaper. Fuad's uncle, the one who had shepherded him out of prison for his father's funeral, presided over the ceremony and sang an anguished *nowheh*, the traditional lamentation for the dead. His voice moved everyone, and in the middle of the ceremony my thoughts wandered. I thought the family should have allowed Fuad to escape that day he was in our midst and had sought our help. If they had let him run, perhaps he would still be alive today.

One year later, in 1989, Javad returned to the authorities to ask where they had buried Fuad. They told him Behesht-e Zahra, Tehran's principal cemetery, which begins on the southern edge of the city and spreads out for miles along the highway that disappears into the desert. Behesht-e Zahra is ostensibly a cemetery, but it looks more like a small suburb or campground, complete with tree-lined roads, a playground, a restaurant, and snack shops; mourners often spend the afternoon there, picnicking among the graves, as their children run about, and people cannot navigate their way around without a guide or a map. The most expansive section is dedicated to soldiers killed in the Iran-Iraq War, and nothing can prepare you for the sight: miles of headstones stretching into the distance, a grotesque horizon of tombs.

We went to the cemetery the next day, weaving through the throngs of mourners, and spent two hours searching for Fuad's grave. He was buried in an old section of the cemetery that had been full for decades, and we realized that the graves of the executed had been scattered throughout the vast cemetery, to prevent a visitor from making any estimate of the number of victims. Many of Behesht-e Zahra's sections are organized by theme: the anti-shah activists killed before the revolution, those killed by the SAVAK during the revolution itself, and so on. The scope of each section is instructive, and reveals the human cost of the violent moments in Iran's history. Had there been a section for the MKO sympathizers and other political prisoners executed after the failed Mersad operation, it would have included between four thousand and five thousand graves, for that is the estimated number that were killed, along with Fuad, in that three-month execution spree in 1988. According to human rights groups and former prisoners, most of the executed were either high school or college students or fresh graduates, and over 10 percent were women.

It was only later, when details emerged through rumor and word of mouth, that we heard of the "trials" conducted before the executions. The proceedings lasted just a few minutes, long enough for the prisoners to be asked questions like Are you a Muslim? What is your organizational affiliation? Do you pray? Is the Holy Koran the word of God? Will you publicly recant historical materialism? If the prisoner—confused, blindfolded, and unaccustomed to religious inquisition—answered incorrectly, there were no more questions, and the execution order was immediately handed down.

If the prisoner claimed belief in Islam, he would be asked if he was willing to collaborate with the regime, and whether he recanted his former beliefs. If the answer was no, again the death sentence; if the answer was yes, the prisoner would be forced to participate in the execution of other prisoners as proof of his conversion. Female prisoners, of which there were many, were reportedly raped before execution to ensure their damnation, for virgins were said to ascend directly to heaven. The overseer of the prison during that bloody time was a conservative named Asadollah Lajevardi. On the ten-year anniversary of the executions, MKO assassins crept up behind Lajevardi, by then an old man, at his drapery shop in the Tehran bazaar and shot him to death with an Uzi submachine gun.

Every time we visited the cemetery, we felt eyes on us, as though we were being watched. The Communists who had been executed had not even been buried in the cemetery, for the regime refused to allow atheists (i.e., nonbelievers, apostates) to be buried alongside Muslims. Their graves were relegated to an abandoned area in southeast Tehran called Khavaran, referred to by religious fundamentalists as the "Accursed Land."

What was the legacy of this war? The borders were unchanged. The world soon forgot. Every time I go to Behesht-e Zahra and gaze at the graves of the war dead, those who will be remembered as a footnote, a numerical estimate, I wonder to myself, Who was the real winner? Not Iran, with its economy in ruins, two-thirds of its provinces devastated, its soldier victims of Saddam's chemical weapons lying in special hospitals, their blistered bodies continually burning. Not Iraq, its population also scarred by war, its Kurds similarly brutalized by nerve gas. Who were the winners then? The arms dealers. The European companies that sold Saddam his chemical weapons, the American firms that sold both sides arms. They amassed fortunes, their bank accounts swollen, their families, in Bonn and Virginia, untouched.

I must linger on the war just a bit longer, because its impact is largely what has shaped current Iranian attitudes about our future and our place in the world. First, the skepticism and mistrust it reinforced in us about America's motives in the region. Imagine if you were an Iranian and watched the boys in your neighborhood board the bus for the front, never to return. Imagine staring in mute horror at the television screen as Saddam rained chemical weapons down on your boys, his death planes guided by U.S. satellite photos. Fast-forward about fifteen years. Now you are watching faded video footage of Donald Rumsfeld shaking Saddam Hussein's hand, smiling at the butcher who made our capital's cemetery a city. Now you are listening to President George W. Bush promise he wants to bring democracy to the Middle East. You are hearing him address the Iranian people in his State of the Union address, telling them that if they stand for their own liberty, America will stand with them. Do you believe him?

It is nearly impossible to reliably estimate the war's toll, on both the two countries' populations and their economies. Both sides sustained about $500 billion in lost oil revenue, military expenditure, and destroyed infrastructure. Both sides minimized their own troop casualties and exaggerated the enemy losses; the only generally accepted figure is that, combined, more than one million Iranians and Iraqis were killed or wounded. More than one hundred thousand soldiers were taken as prisoners of war, and the fighting produced about 2.5 million refugees.

CHAPTER SIX

Strange Times, My Darling

AYATOLLAH KHOMEINI DIED ON A TEMPERATE SATURDAY, June 3, 1989. For several consecutive nights, the evening news had been reporting that the ayatollah was ill. That Saturday, I turned the television on to hear the broadcaster asking us all to pray for him, specifically the special prayer reserved for the very ill. He must be dying, I thought, if we are to say this prayer. The next morning, I woke up much earlier than usual and rolled over to switch on the radio. After two turns of the dial, I knew he was gone. If you are in a Muslim nation and suddenly every radio station is broadcasting the Koran ceaselessly, you don't need an announcement to tell you the leader has died.

With his passing, as with his arrival from exile, Tehran descended into full-blown chaos. Millions of Iranians—estimates range from four to nine million—donned the black garb of Shia mourning and streamed into the streets and highways of the city, moving south toward the Behesht-e Zahra cemetery, where the ayatollah would be buried alongside the martyrs of the Iraq war. Women swathed in black chadors beat their chests rhythmically, wailing in lament the way Shia have mourned their martyrs and their dead for centuries.

No city's police force is properly equipped to cope with such an overwhelming sea of humanity. We sat transfixed before the television, watching the thronging whorls of black, able only to imagine the dirt and sweat that caked people's skin as they moved en masse toward the ayatollah's coffin, nearly hysterical in their eagerness to touch or tear off a piece of his white *kafan*, or burial shroud. The security forces doused the crowd with fire hoses, hoping to calm them and thus stand a chance of actually bearing the ayatollah to his burial site. "This nation, what will it do without you?" the crowd chanted, heaving forward and surrounding the refrigerated truck.

When the motor of an army helicopter cut through the air, the black mass lightened as mourners turned their faces up to the sky. The truck was blocked off and the coffin was transferred from it to the helicopter, then ferried straight to the grave site, where another keening crowd awaited. An intrepid photographer caught what happened next, capturing another of the twentieth century's most enduring images: of Ayatollah Khomeini's shrouded body slipping out of the plywood coffin, his leg dangling out. The crowd had descended on the coffin, people trampling one another in a frenzy to tear off a piece of the shroud; in the mayhem, the coffin gave. It was rumored later that MKO members in the crowd were trying to stab his corpse. Shots rang out as troops rushed to rescue the body and lift it back into the helicopter. Mourners clung to the helicoptor's skids, and it rose up and down several times to shake them off.

Several hours later, multiple army helicopters returned to the grave site with the body, now in a metal casket. One descended swiftly to the area where the mourners had been pushed back, where Ayatollah Khomeini's son, his successor as supreme leader, Ayatollah Ali Khamenei, and Akbar Hashemi Rafsanjani, the enduring heavyweight of Iranian politics, now stood. They surveyed the reconstructed security barriers around the plain grave site and concluded that the body could be buried without it being lost again. The body was removed from the box, for the Shia bury their dead only in a shroud. Again mourners scaled the barriers and flung themselves toward the site. The circling helicopters blasted them with water, and finally, in a cacophony of screams and motors, in the dust thrown up by the water hoses, Ayatollah Khomeini, hero of the *mustazafin* (the dispossessed), founder of the Islamic state, charismatic icon of Third World struggle, was finally laid to rest.

The broadcasters on state television sobbed through the news that evening, but people's reactions were not so uniform. Many, like the tens of thousand who kept vigil around his grave that night, were truly desolate. Others were more frightened than anything else, worried that the ayatollah's death would result in anarchy and street fighting. Some were more thoughtful. They dared not say so, but they hoped that with his death the country might moderate and change course.

The charismatic ayatollah who had mesmerized Iranians with his deceptively simple cries of "The Shah must go!" was himself now gone. In his place a clique of revolutionaries—all of them lacking Ayatollah Khomeini's iconic stature, his commanding presence—presided over a shell-shocked nation beginning to wonder, The revolution, this eight-year war, was it all worth it? Since the war was over, the government had turned its attention to pressing matters it had neglected during wartime, such as making sure Iranians did not date or watch unseemly television.

Nervous about their grip over the country and the direction of an only partly consolidated revolution, the new leadership imposed social restrictions with a new vigor. Perhaps if Iranians were cut off from the outside world, perhaps if couples were not allowed to frequent cafés, the still nascent Islamic Republic would somehow wrestle people's affections? Whether the objective was to instill fear and dissuade dissent or to impose an unpopular and harsh interpretation of Islam, the result was the same: the politics of the regime nosed into our lives, followed us into our living rooms, turned our everyday existence into a cat-and-mouse game of evading the authorities.

The *komiteh,* or morality police, harassed all Iranians—Muslims as well as Iranian Christians and Jews, old people as well as the young—but they preyed upon women with a special enthusiasm. Slowly we learned to cope with the obstacle course that was public space. Dating couples socializing ahead of marriage, for example, would borrow a young niece or nephew on their evenings out, to appear as a family and pass through checkpoints unmolested. We monitored everything from our personalities to our wardrobes, careful not to express opinions in public, to wear socks with our sandals. But often the harassment was arbitrary and senseless, and thus impossible to anticipate. When most look back on those years, their memories are of antagonistic scenes that left them with headaches and a reservoir of resentment. Some recall encounters so wounding that neither their bodies nor their spirits ever quite recovered.

Sometimes it seemed the *komiteh* terrorized us because they didn't know what else to do. None of us did, really. The poet Ahmad Shamlou, in one of his best-loved poems, catalogs many of the brutalities we witnessed in the early days of the revolution. Each stanza ends with "strange times, my darling." The year or two directly after the war were nothing if not strange. It felt as though we were barreling ahead into darkness, uncertain of our direction but unable to slow down.

Some Iranians who had left the country during the war returned for brief visits, to assess the evolving climate. Some of them, like my friend Soraya, found that the *komitehs* had turned to raiding their fellow Iranians, in place of the Iraqi front. Her parents lived in a small, lush village near the Caspian Sea, and just a couple of weeks after the war ended she flew home and drove out to visit them, along with her fiancé and two of their male friends. They took a circuitous route, to explore a bit along the way, and passed through the northwestern province where the MKO had launched its failed operation several days prior.

While their car idled at a small-town intersection, a *komiteh* member strode up and curtly instructed them to open the trunk. One of the friends, instead of staying silent as people would learn to do in the years to come, snapped back, "Open it yourself." Before they knew it, the man from the *komiteh* was summoning reinforcements and directing them toward a makeshift building that served as a courthouse, interrogation center, and *komiteh* barracks all in one. The *komiteh* separated Soraya from the men and began interrogating them separately. Once their identifying information was jotted down, the authorities—or the loose assembly of an interrogator, the *komiteh,* and a revolutionary judge, which passed for the authorities—concluded that they must be MKO.

Soraya, they said suspiciously, was too literate to be just an ordinary Iranian girl passing through the province to visit her parents. She had filled out her interrogation form in beautiful handwriting, with cogent, reasoned prose. They waved the form in her face, as though it were a bloody knife bearing her fingerprints. When she explained that she had studied law, that she was trained to think and write in such terms, her interrogators shook their heads skeptically. When they learned that one of the men in the group had been studying abroad in Britain, they needed no more evidence. They had a cabal on their hands.

For two days, they kept them there. Soraya was alone in a filthy, empty room, in a separate complex that they locked her into and abandoned at night. After forty-eight hours, confirmations began coming in from Tehran. Soraya was indeed a staffer at the national television network. The friends' identities also checked out. None of their superiors or professors knew them to have any links to the MKO at all. You might imagine that the whole debacle would stop there. But why should it? They were arrested on a whim, detained on unfounded suspicion; it was clear they were being harassed for the sake of it. It was an opportunity for the *komiteh* to vent their anger at the MKO, at two Iranians guilty of the opportunity to leave the country, at a woman guilty of being educated and in the company of men who were not her brothers.

The judge, a slovenly cleric seated behind a makeshift table, summoned them into his room and called them up one by one. "First send me Engilis," he said, referring to the one who had studied abroad. Next he called up Soraya, who was a truly beautiful young woman. "Isn't it a shame," he whispered, "for a girl as intelligent as you to go to prison, to run around with these young men? If you confess, I'll take you as a temporary wife myself."

In the interrogation sessions, they separated them again and tried to force Soraya to confess to having sexual relations with all the men. "They've all said they've been with you," the interrogator sneered. "And as for your supposed fiancé, he says he just sleeps with you, that you're nothing to him." By that point she was nearly hysterical, from the sleepless nights, kept awake by her fear and by the buzz of mosquitoes. "Bring him here," she cried tearfully. "Have him say that to my face."

In the end, the judge summoned them for one last session. Although they'd failed to be spies, failed to be MKO, failed to be any threat to the regime or the country, they could at least be punished for flouting Islamic law by appearing together in public, unmarried and unrelated.

"You," he said, nodding toward Soraya, "forty lashes." She stared at him in shock. He was eating, a plate of *chelo-kabob* glistening with butter before him.

"Are you a judge?" she hissed. "Because if you are, why don't you finish eating before handing down a sentence. Or do you want me to be lashed so badly you can't even wait until you're done? Why is it that all you know of the Koran is to lash and to whip? Did you skip that whole part at the beginning, about the mercy and the compassion? Do you not know that, under Islamic law, I cannot be lashed except for by a woman?"

He looked stung. Her last point was unarguable. Under sharia,

Islamic law, only a woman can inflict corporal punishment on another woman. He was livid at being dressed down by a woman, corrected about a punishment that he meted out so freely, over his lunch. There was no woman on hand to lash Soraya, so the judge took his wrath out on her fiancé. "Eighty for him," he barked. "And take her with you, so she can watch."

They took Soraya's fiancé into the next room and laid him down on the bare floor. One of the men took out a cable, and of course he did not hold a Koran under his arm, to soften the blows, as he is meant to. For in the spirit of the sharia, the deterrent quality of a lashing lies in humiliation, not in wounding of the flesh; most dominant schools of interpretation maintain that the lasher must hold a Koran under the arm with which he is lashing, so that he never forgets this. In this case, the *komitehs* paid no attention to the spirit of anything except their vengefulness.

After the thirtieth blow, blood soaked through the fiancé's shirt. After the fiftieth, he began to cry out, and it was then that Soraya began pounding at the door of the judge's room. "You will be punished for this, I promise you!" she screamed. "If I don't come back one day and kill you myself, somehow you will be punished, you animal."

And that, I think, illustrates how the *komitehs* operated for many years. They harassed people because they felt like it, looked for pretexts to intimidate them, and, when they found none, made them up. A bitter look, a misplaced word, the most casual defense of self could provoke them into great rage, and before you knew it, you were three days into an interrogation, being accused of anything from adultery to treason. It was during that period, I believe, the strange times just after the war, when Iranians began to notice the emotional nicks inflicted by the presence of the *komiteh* in their lives. Husbands were humiliated before their wives, mothers before their sons. Often people did not relate their encounters to one another, preferring to keep their shame private, but just as nearly all Iranians had a relative or friend killed in the war or in the MKO executions, everyone also knew someone close who had been arrested, lashed, or disgraced in some public way at the hands of the *komiteh*.

Sometimes the *komiteh* campaigns supplied fresh material to our already darkened humor. Perhaps it was the saving grace of these strange times that occasionally the morality police made everyone—both enforcer and the enforced—confront the absurdity of their position. My mother and daughters never let me forget what transpired one winter when we tried to go skiing in Dizin, the spectacular resort that lies about an hour outside Tehran. We had begun spending several days there each year, so the girls could learn how to ski. Skiing being a sport that requires many layers of clothing, it was deemed marginally acceptable by the government. That year we decided not to drive our car and instead to take one of the buses from downtown Tehran directly to the slopes. We set out before dawn, and the girls and I boarded the women's bus, waving to Javad, who disappeared onto the men's. At one of the checkpoints on the windy, snow-dusted road to Dizin, I reminded the driver that my daughters and I wouldn't be returning on the same bus, so he shouldn't include us in the head count. Something about this remark aroused suspicion, and the officer at the checkpoint called us off the bus.

"My husband is on the men's bus," I explained, "and we're staying for a few days." From the steamy window of the checkpoint kiosk, I could see the men's bus snaking up the road into the mountains. There was no way to reach Javad and have him confirm my story. "*Khanum*, you need your parents' permission to sleep out overnight," replied the commanding officer with a shrug.

I gazed at him, dumbfounded. The girls were standing beside me. "I have two daughters," I said. "Of course I don't live with my parents. The men's bus is gone, so there's nothing I can do."

"I'm sorry," he said obstinately. "I can't let the bus depart."

Twenty female pairs of eyes stared at us in irritation through the windows of the bus.

"This is absurd," I said. "It's not fair to the other people on that bus."

"There's only one solution," he sighed. To send us back to Tehran? I wondered.

"I have to call your mother and see if you have permission to go skiing."

By that point I was livid, but I thought of the women sitting on the bus in the freezing cold and agreed.

"Just let me talk to her first," I said. My mother had developed a heart condition, and I thought that if a policeman phoned her at dawn about me, she would probably have a heart attack on the spot.

And that is how I was forced, at the age of forty-five, to dial up my mother and say, "Maman, can you please tell this man that I'm allowed to go skiing?"

He took the phone from me. "Madam, are you aware that your daughter, by the name of Shirin, will not be returning home for four nights?" She said yes, he hung up, and we were nearly out the door when I paused.

"By the way," I asked, "how did you know that was really my mother? How do you know it wasn't a fake number?"

He looked shocked. Two sharp elbows simultaneously jabbed into my sides. Negar shot me a look that said, Did you really need to remind him?

He shrugged. "Well, the law says I have to call, so I called."

As we boarded the bus, giggling, and drove up through the ravine, I looked at the pine trees peeking out from the snow and thought about what ghosts our laws had become. The people who embody the law—lawyers, judges, policemen—are the ones who uphold the meaning of legality, because otherwise laws are just words on paper.

When we returned to Tehran, my mother teased me for an entire month. "Next time they call me, Shirin," she said, "I'm going to tell them no!"

Often the restrictions women faced in the early nineties culminated as our skiing mishap had—in unpleasant, time-sapping confrontations in which young men spoke rudely to women old enough to be their mothers. Just as often, however, the morality police conducted themselves with a frightening, thuggish authority. Certain squares around Tehran became notorious for their *komiteh* patrols, and the methods grew more disturbingly efficient with time, to keep up with women's techniques of evasion. If a woman strolling down the street noticed a *komiteh* patrol in the distance, for example, she would swiftly pull her *hejab* forward over her hair and wipe off any makeup. So the

The Society for the Defense of Children's Rights.

morality police soon expanded to include plainclothes women who hid walkie-talkies under their chadors and would radio in to summon the male *komiteh* and their vans to round up unsuspecting women.

For women, public space—from the produce stand to the park to the bus stop—became fraught with uncertainty. You simply did not know where, at what hour, and under what pretext you might be harassed, and often the confrontations with the *komiteh* turned alarming. After I was arrested myself once or twice for *bad hejabi*, or improper Islamic dress, I concluded that there was little one could do for protection against a state that simply wished to impose a climate of fear. And that was the ultimate aim, I suspected, a fear so pervasive that it would keep women at home, the place where traditional Iranian men believed they should be.

I was arrested for the first time on a sunny spring afternoon in Ramsar, a small town near the Caspian Sea, where we sometimes went to celebrate the Persian New Year. I was already wearing a long coat, long, baggy pants, and a head scarf when a police officer approached me in the town square. "Get on the minibus," he said to me roughly, pointing to a white van parked nearby. When I protested, he grabbed my arm, dragged me across the street, and shoved me onto the bus. Three other unfortunate women were already huddled on the seats. One was a retired schoolteacher, arrested for wearing slippers.

"My feet are swollen, I can't wear shoes!" she yelled at the officer, who was scanning the square for more prey. "Where," she continued, "does it say in the Koran that wearing slippers is a crime?"

The louder she yelled, the more agitated the officer became, and soon he gave up on filling the minivan and simply drove us to police headquarters. They installed us in a room and told us to remain there until a female officer came to "guide" us. In the traditionalist notion of *amr be maruf va nahi az monker*, pious Muslims believe it is their duty to uphold virtue and discourage vice through policing the behavior of those in the community.

The door clanked open, and an eighteen-year-old girl in a black chador strode in. Our guide had arrived, and from her terse, colloquial tone, it was clear she was illiterate.

"I am going to recite a poem from Hazrat-e Fatemeh to you," she announced. Fatemeh was the daughter of the prophet Mohammed, an Islamic paragon of female devotion and piety.

"Oh women!" she began. "Fatemeh addresses you thus: the most precious ornament of woman is her *hejab*." She stopped and scanned our faces, seeming quite proud of herself.

"Excuse me, but Hazrat-e Fatemeh was not a poet," the schoolteacher pointed out. The guide pretended not to hear her and made a few vague remarks about Judgment Day, heaven, and hell. She seemed surprised when we didn't realize that her desultory sermon had ended.

"Well, what are you waiting for? You can go now," she said. We had been officially guided.

As I sat there on the dirty floor of a coastal town's *komiteh* headquarters, listening to this eighteen-year-old girl's harangue, it struck me that our guide was a true phenomenon of the Islamic Republic. Under the shah's Iran, this young woman would have been sitting in her house, washing or chopping something. The government could not have reached out to her even if it had wanted to, for her traditional, provincial parents would have used her honor as a pretext to keep her at home. This revolution reached out to women like the guide. In its early days, the Islamic regime needed the votes of women from traditional families and lured them to come out to the ballot boxes. If you vote, you've helped Islam, the clergy told them. This gave women from traditional families an unprecedented self-confidence. They realized that contrary to what they had assumed, they mattered to something beyond their homes. Their votes counted. They could play a role.

In those years, elections functioned mostly as a popular rubber stamp of the system's legitimacy. Even under the shah, the ballot box was an alien concept to most Iranians. The court usually preapproved the list of candidates, and no one was surprised by the outcome, given the lack of serious competition. One of my relatives who served as a member of parliament under the shah hadn't even visited the district he was supposedly elected from more than twice. People had no sense of what an election was all about, and that's why when they were herded up to vote in the Islamic Republic's elections, they still understood little about the process. I remember television broadcasting interviews of people in line during those early revolutionary days, and when the announcer would ask, "Who are you voting for?" lots of people simply said, "For the victory of Islam, of course!"

People were unfamiliar with the revolutionaries on the ballot, but they heeded the call of the mosques—"Vote so the Imam-e Zaman [the twelfth Shia imam] will be pleased with you!"—and turned out on elections days. They could choose freely among the unknown candidates, and they believed in the legitimacy of the process, though they were perhaps indifferent to its outcome. As time passed, awareness of the electoral process grew; people slowly understood that they were selecting representatives who would legislate policies affecting the minutiae of their lives, and they paid more attention to their choices. Sadly enough, in the early nineties, when Iranians began to grasp that elections granted them a say in how the country was run, a law was passed giving an unelected clerical body known as the Guardian Council vetting power over candidates in both parliamentary and presidential elections; with that law, Iranians lost their right to choose their representatives freely. Elections remained competitive and never took on the farcical character of the vote in neighboring dictatorships, but they also ceased to reflect the true will of the people.

For women who were either illiterate or the first generation to see the inside of a classroom, however, the very act of voting remained powerfully symbolic. It was this conviction that a woman could play a role in society that enabled the provincial girl of eighteen to bellow a shoddy sermon at me, a onetime judge, a woman in her forties. I would not have been surprised if the girl had female cousins attending college, for in those years the universities had become Islamic, dedicated to the education of women like this. Girls went to class in *hejabs* and sat in separate classrooms; even the lunch tables in the cafeteria were segregated. If the universities had been dens of sin in the shah's Iran, what were they now? Rehabilitated! Healthy! There was no pretext left for the patriarchs to keep their daughters out of school, and they slowly found themselves in classrooms, and away from their parents in dormitories in Tehran. A generation of women whose mothers had been tethered to the house found themselves in cities, reading books. Slowly, it became fashionable for the daughters of traditional families to attend college.

There was no talk yet of feminism, of course; "feminist" was still a pejorative word fundamentalists used against anyone who questioned the discriminatory legal code, such as myself. It was too soon, still, for a grassroots women's rights campaign. The majority of women still would not support such notions, because they were only becoming exposed to the horizon of opportunity, to the question of their own rights. Sometimes consciousness emerges slowly; on the way, it mistakes bullying for authority, and access to opportunity for equality of rights. But that day I saw the process beginning. Not without some pain, of course, for the current that would propel the guide into college was the same one that had swept me out of my judgeship.

The extension of university education to a whole caste of women naturally resulted in major tension within families. A girl who has been encouraged to vote and who is attending college is less inclined to dumbly obey the instructions of her father. Our next-door neighbors provided me with a vivid, long-running illustration of this phenomenon. Just before the revolution, the very religious father married his eldest daughter off to an even more pious *bazaari*. (The term refers to a trader or merchant, usually of deeply traditional background.) The *bazaari* promptly forced her to wear the chador, then forbade her to visit her own parents unaccompanied. The poor girl was wretched, spending long days marooned at home, waiting for her extremist husband to return in the evening and drive her over to her parents'. They fought bitterly. The parents knew I had been a judge and was also a practicing Muslim, so they often invited me over to advise them on how to help their daughter.

It took all of my efforts not to yell at this conflicted man, anxious about his daughter's happiness but ultimately loyal to his honor, which, like most traditional men, he defined through her virtue. In the middle of our sessions, I would hear sobs echoing from the second daughter's bedrooms. "Why is she upset?" I finally asked one evening. "She wants to go to college," the mother said, casting a baleful look at her husband. "But her father won't let her."

"What?" he said defensively. "Should I send my daughter to go sit in classes with women with loose hair, so that boys can flirt with her?"

The revolution came too late for the second daughter. She was consigned to a man less rigid than her older sister's husband but still adamant that no wife of his would abandon the kitchen for the classroom. The youngest daughter's high school graduation coincided neatly with the Islamic Revolution. The father secured a plummy government job after the revolution, for in those days ostentatious piety sufficiently filled out a résumé. Now an official in the Islamic Republic, a theocracy that segregated classrooms to preserve morality at the universities, he could no longer cling to his spurious arguments on the corrupting nature of education. The youngest daughter started medical school and married one of her classmates, a man of her own choosing.

Throughout the nineties, the number of women with college degrees rose steadily, and eventually women began to outnumber men in universities by a slim margin. This was no small achievement for a Middle Eastern country with a culture still patriarchal to its core. In neighboring Afghanistan, the Taliban forbade women to read; across the water in Saudi Arabia, women were banned from driving. But what the Islamic Republic had managed terrified its founders. Traditionalist clerics sought unsuccessfully to reverse the dangerous trend by imposing a gender quota system on the universities.

Unfortunately, equal access to education did not translate into equality of rights or professional opportunity. The drawn-out war had eventually forced the system to mobilize women, and they were recruited to work in mass laundries and kitchens that serviced the war front. But at that time, the traditionalists permitted women back into the public domain only in areas where it served them. Managerial and decision-making positions, as well as whole institutions such as the judiciary, were still largely off-limits. Women like my next-door neighbor's daughter whose worlds expanded with entrance to a university found that it contracted upon their exit. The Islamic Republic simply could not produce enough jobs to keep up with its fast-growing workforce, and the jobs that were available went mainly to men. Though educated women outnumbered educated men, the rate of women's unemployment was three times higher. The franchise of higher education did not chip away at gender discrimination, enshrined in our culture as well as our institutions. But it instilled something in Iranian women that will in the long run, I believe, transform Iran: a visceral consciousness of their oppression.

All these educated women emerging from Iranian universities were no longer content to slip back into their traditional roles, to shelve their degrees and pretend that their expectations of life were unchanged. This new consciousness, and the disappointment of unmet expectations—unmet because their fathers and husbands had not undergone a similar transformation—resulted in painful, sometimes tragic clashes with family. I remember reading in the newspaper one day, years later, about the self-immolation of the daughter of a Friday sermon leader in the province of Azerbaijan. Unhappy in her marriage, the woman had tried to divorce her husband. Her father, as orthodox a cleric as they came, refused. Facing a lifetime as a hostage in an awful marriage, the woman doused herself with gasoline and lit herself ablaze. Perhaps, I thought, if this woman had come of age under the shah, had inherited the same conservative obedience of that social background, she would have stayed in that bad marriage, rather than perishing in a pyre of her own making. She would have been taught only that this is how the world is, that it is women's lot to cope.

The Islamic Republic had inadvertently championed traditional women, yet it has also left them ruthlessly vulnerable, for they had been given a new awareness of their rights but only crude tools with which to advance them. Some believe that living under these conditions, being kept in the dark, ignorant of possibilities, is a blessing for such women. At least ignorance produces a shadowy contentment. The Friday prayer leader's daughter was not a singular case. The suicide rate among women rose after the Islamic Revolution, commonly taking the form of self-immolation. This tragic exhibitionism, I'm convinced, is women's way of forcing their community to confront the cruelty of their oppression. Otherwise, would it not simply be easier to overdose on pills in a dark room?

About two years into the postwar period, the Islamic Republic quietly changed course. Even the most militant, bearded ideologue could see where the revolution's policies—the marginalization of women, the pro-natal agenda that banned contraception—had taken the country. It was fairly clear by then that the Shia revolution would not be sweeping the region. It was clear that the Iranian economy could no longer support a burgeoning population, whose growth rate had jumped to the highest in the world. Iran, the system's leaders concluded, needed to integrate into the world economy or risk devolving into a truly impoverished Third World nation. Privatization, a new focus on manufacturing rather than agriculture, and attracting foreign investment all became new priorities for the state. There was just one hitch: Iran didn't have the knowledge and human-resource base to undertake such ambitions. The Islamic Republic had wrapped women in veils and stuck them in the kitchen. Now it needed to rebuild itself after a devastating war, and it needed them back.

As part of this involuntary pragmatism, in 1992 the judiciary relented and permitted women to begin practicing law. The Iranian Bar Association granted me a license, and I set up an office in the downstairs flat of our building and began seeing clients. Commercial and trade cases filled my days, though occasionally I would accept a pro bono case, usually something politically sensitive. In short order, after attending court with my clients and litigating a number of cases, I saw that this was a justice system in name only. I had figured that at least in commercial cases, the politics and ideology of the new Islamic Republic would not seep into its jurisdiction. Instead, corruption prevailed. As a lawyer, it was my job to advance my client's case—to win back his money or his property, or to defend him against unjust allegations. More than once a client showed up in my office beaming, pleased to report that the prosecution had agreed to settle in exchange for an under-the-table bribe. What was the point of knowing case law and preparing a defense? Indeed, what was the point of showing up in a courtroom, pretending to act out the legal process, when it all just came down to deal making in the court chambers? On two occasions, when the judge had nothing left to say, he declared that strands of my hair were poking out, and adjourned the court on grounds of my *bad hejabi*.

We had managed for years without two incomes, I reasoned, and could do so again. I was working not simply for the sake of a salary but to feel fulfilled professionally, to apply my knowledge and make a contribution to the country where I had chosen to remain. By accepting commercial cases, I was put in the position of either abandoning my principles or failing my clients. Neither was acceptable to me. It was at this point that I chose to give up the law as a job that earned me income and to begin exclusively taking on pro bono cases, where I could at least showcase the injustice of the Islamic Republic's laws. It was a system whose laws needed to go on trial before they could be changed.

I had to choose cases, I realized, that illustrated the tragic repercussions of the theocracy's legal discrimination against women. I could recite a litany of objectionable laws—a woman's life is worth half as much as a man's, child custody after infancy goes automatically to the father—until I was out of breath. But a personal story is more powerful than any dry summary of why a given law should be changed. To attract people's attention, to solicit their sympathies and convince them that these laws were not simply unfair but actively pathological, I had to tell stories. Iranian culture, for all its preoccupation with shame and honor, with all its resulting patriarchal codes, retains an acute sensitivity to injustice. The revolution against the shah, after all, had premised itself on the ethos of fighting *zolm*, or oppression; it was a revolution conducted in the name of the *mustazafin*, the dispossessed. People had to see how the dispossessed had now become the dispossessors.

CHAPTER SEVEN

From the Living Room to the Courtroom

LEILA FATHI DISAPPEARED ONE SUNNY DAY IN THE SUMMER of 1996 while picking wildflowers in the hills behind her village, near the northwestern Kurdish city of Sanandaj. Her parents, like many in the region, struggled to get by, and eleven-year-old Leila was collecting the wild plants and flowers the family would then dry and sell in the local bazaar. She and her cousin had set out with their woven baskets in the late morning and had interrupted their picking to play among the tall grasses. Growing up near Sanandaj, where people picnicked outdoors, held weddings under the open sky, and danced alongside the riverbanks, they ran about as though the hills were an extension of their tiny living room, with nothing like the intuitive watchfulness of urban children. Bent over filling her skirt with petals, Leila didn't notice the three men approaching. They emerged from the back side of the hill, moving quietly until they were almost atop her, and then closed in swiftly. One twisted her thin arms behind her back, while another tried to clasp her thrashing legs together. Her cousin managed to escape, and he hid behind a tree, watching the men drag a fighting, kicking Leila

Speaking to children at the Society for the Defense of Children's Rights.

over to a slope. He watched them tear off her peasant skirt and rape her, strike a fatal blow to her head, and then hurl her battered body over a cliff in the craggy hillside.

The local police arrested the three men, but after the prime suspect confessed to the crime, he mysteriously hung himself in prison. Odd that in a prison where inmates are not even allowed to wear watches, he had conveniently found a meter of braided rope, just the length for hanging. The other two suspects denied complicity, but the court found them guilty of rape and sentenced them to death.

I mentioned earlier that under the Islamic penal code instituted after the revolution, a man's life is worth twice that of a woman. In most Islamic countries, laws determining compensation apply only in financial cases, such as inheritance. The Islamic Republic, however, applies compensation, or "blood money" provisions, in criminal cases. Under Islamic law, the family of a victim of homicide or manslaughter has the right to choose between legal punishment and financial compensation, referred to as blood money. Many Islamic scholars hold that blood money should be blind to gender, but Iran practices a discriminatory interpretation. Under the Iranian code, the worth of a woman's life equals half of a man's, a point that often leads to grotesque legal judgments that effectively punish the victim. In this instance, the judge ruled that the "blood money" for the two men was worth more than the life of the murdered eleven-year-old girl, and he demanded that her family come up with thousands of dollars to finance their executions.

Leila's father sold all of his few worldly possessions, including the little clay hut where his family slept. Homeless but convinced that they would at least reclaim their honor, they offered the money to the court. It was not enough. The family took to sleeping at the shrine of Ayatollah Khomeini, a vast mausoleum on the road to Qom, while trying to raise the remaining cash. First Leila's father volunteered to sell a kidney, but his organ was rejected because of his past drug abuse. Next Leila's brother offered his up, but the doctor refused because he was handicapped by polio. "Why," asked the doctor, "are you two so insistent on selling your kidneys?" Out poured the tale. They could not return to their village, they explained, stained by the shame of Leila's rape. Family honor rests on the virtue of women, and nothing less than the perpetrators' execution could erase their shame.

Horrified by this bizarre tale, the doctor wrote to the head of the judiciary and threatened to report the case to an international organization, Doctors Without Borders, unless the state treasury made up the difference needed for the execution. The judiciary chief agreed, but in a further unbelievable twist, just days before the scheduled execution one of the convicts escaped from prison, and, in the meantime, Leila's disconsolate family had erected a ramshackle cloth tent on the sidewalk outside the courthouse. The family was shocked to learn that the court had reopened the case. Perhaps it was because the ambiguities inherent in the Iranian legal system mean that even a closed case always remains subject to further review. Perhaps, as Leila's family claimed, it was because one of the accused used a relative, a conservative member of parliament, to influence the outcome. The case was unraveling.

It was at this point that I heard about the case and decided to take a look at the file. At first I was skeptical. Criminal justice in the postrevolutionary legal system was flawed; it denied female victims of violence equal restitution. But the case of Leila's family suggested that it was effectively pathological, capable of destroying the livelihoods of those who petitioned for justice on behalf of their victimized loved ones. I paid a visit to the family at their tent outside the courthouse, and after listening to their account of the long, sordid tale, I agreed to represent them.

The outlines of the case were stark, and I constructed a simple, elegant defense: it was unjust for a girl to be raped and killed, and for her family to have lost every possession and become homeless through the legal proceedings that followed; it was unjust that the victims were now being victimized further by the law. "Do not criticize Islamic law," the judge sternly warned me in court. "I'm only asking if justice has been served," I retorted.

As the session neared its close, someone whispered in my ear that Leila's brothers had concealed kitchen knives in their coats and were planning to attack the remaining defendant as he left the court. I asked for a recess and called the boys out into the hall.

"Please," I said, "please give me a chance to see what I can do in court first."

Both of them sat on a bench and wept. "If we had paid a professional assassin *half* of what we paid the court," one of them cried, "justice would have been carried out. Now we're homeless, while one of them is free and the other is about to walk."

"I know," I whispered. "I know. But let's try."

Over the course of the proceedings, the court acquitted both defendants, overturned the acquittals, and then relaunched the investigation. The family's grief slowly descended into madness. Leila's mother took to sitting outside the courthouse in a white funeral shroud, holding a placard that described her daughter's violation. During one trial, she threatened to set herself on fire, and began screaming profanities at the court. As though the whole proceeding was not dramatic enough, the judge held her in contempt of court and filed legal charges against her that took us weeks of mediation to settle.

It would tire your patience if I detailed the legal proceedings any further, but suffice it to say that the case was not resolved, and remains open to this day. I did not succeed in getting the legal system to mete out anything approximating justice, but I do think we accomplished something else: we made a national showcase of the flaws in Iranian law concerning the rights of women and children. The case swiftly turned into a public issue, so much so that candidates in Leila's province ran on platforms that included stances on her case. The Iranian press took on Leila's story as an egregious illustration of the social problems of the Islamic Republic.

The trial reverberated long after the final court session. It played itself out in the newspapers as well as the courtroom, and the publicity established my reputation as a lawyer whose work focused on the rights of women and children. I learned very quickly that one of the most powerful tools at the disposal of the legally powerless was the media. My prominence in turn made me more effective at defending my clients, because the judge knew that both he and the judiciary would be forced to justify their decision in the court of public opinion. Oftentimes they simply did not care, but at those times I reminded myself that raising people's awareness of their rights was in itself a contribution.

In the course of the dark months when I watched Leila's family fall apart in despair, as the case garnered more attention, I was struck by how few women even knew that the legal system discriminated against them so severely. Most women had some sense of the laws governing child custody and divorce, because at some point exiting a marriage occurs to many. But by and large, murder or accidental death did not touch the lives of the majority of women; they had no occasion to hear or learn about what sort of fate might lay in store for them, what sort of legal morass awaited them, should they be so unlucky as to have an incident like Leila's befall their family.

I decided to write an article for the magazine *Iran-e Farda,* in approachable language, rather than in an overly intellectual or legalistic style, that would set out in stark terms women's inferior status in the penal code. The section of the code devoted to blood money, *diyeh,* holds that if a man suffers an injury that damages his testicles, he is entitled to compensation equal to a woman's life. I put it this way in my article: if a professional woman with a PhD is run over in the street and killed and an illiterate thug gets one of his testicles injured in a fight, the value of her life and his damaged testicle are equal. There is a vulgar expression in Persian that conveys deep contempt for someone: "You're not even worth one of my testicles." I politely invoked this in my article, to explain in terms no Iranian could mistake just how outrageous these laws were, how they treated women as nonpeople. In the end I posed a question: Is this really how the Islamic Republic regards its women?

The article both titillated and electrified literate Tehran. The editor had published it eagerly, aware that it would, like much of the magazine's content, provoke the hard-line judiciary. The issue sold out immediately, and people showed up at the magazine's offices, begging for even a photocopy of the article. I was stunned. I had expected that it might circulate widely, but I'd never thought it would resound this way throughout the city. A hard-line member of parliament threatened me publicly, telling reporters, "Someone stop this woman, or we'll shut her up ourselves." When I heard this, I realized for the first time that the system might actually fear me and the growing public resonance with my work.

In 1996, the year Leila's case went to court, the Islamic regime tolerated little criticism of its repressive ways. The suppression of political dissent had mellowed some from the early, brutal days of the revolution, when the papers were full of the photos and names of the summarily executed, but the system still punished any perceived challenge to its authority severely. We lived with daily examples of even prominent grand ayatollahs who had been defrocked (unheard of in Shia Islam) or placed under house arrest for speaking out against executions and harsh forms of criminal punishment, such as the chopping off of hands. If the system was willing to disgrace and effectively imprison distinguished senior theologians who had participated actively in the revolution, why should it hesitate for a moment in punishing me, a nonrevolutionary, a noncleric, and, as a woman, a nonperson?

I was nervous. While I was arguing Leila's case, the judge repeatedly accused me of speaking against Islam and its sacred laws. In the politico-religious worldview of such traditionalists, a person who challenges Islam is easily considered an apostate. And the power of interpretation—the power to differentiate between a respectful criticism of a worldly law and an attack on a holy tenet—was in their hands. I was fighting on their battlefield. And I could not simply pull out a copy of the Universal Declaration of Human Rights and wave it in the faces of clerics who found seventh-century penal practice instructive. To argue that Leila's family should not have to finance the execution of her killer or to argue that a woman's life should equal a man's before the law, I too had to draw on Islamic principles and precedents in Islamic law.

*M*y two daughters were growing old enough that they came home from school each day with a barrage of questions. *Thud.* They would toss their backpacks in the hallway. *Thud thud.* They would run down the hall, fingers sticky from a snack on the way home. Navigating the Islamic Republic as a woman was getting more tricky, and so was navigating Islamic Republic motherhood. Maman, is it really wrong

My daughters, Negar and Nargess.

for me to go in front of my male cousins without a veil? Maman, is America truly the source of all that is toxic in the world? Maman, was Mossadegh really a bad man? It was a delicate balance, trying to teach my daughters progressive values and the emptiness behind the revolutionary dogma they were fed in school, while ensuring that they learned and superficially obeyed all that dogma anyway, so they could pass through the education system. "A lot of this is simply wrong," I would usually say, "but you need to study it anyway, so you can pass your exams and go to college."

My husband, Javad, as usual, left these delicate lessons to me. Just as he left the cooking, the shopping, the cleaning, the balancing of the checkbook, and the shuttling of the girls to and from their classes to me. With the caseload I was taking on, balancing the attention the girls needed at home and my work was getting harder.

And now the girls didn't need just bedtime stories anymore. They needed our guidance in dealing with adolescence in Tehran, with all its lures and chaos. "Just tell me if you need any help," Javad would say. And that struck me as most unfair of all, because I certainly never waited for him to ask, "Shirin *jan*, can you please cook dinner tonight?" I cooked dinner every single night because it was obvious to me that it was my responsibility. This was the running theme of our arguments. He wanted me to tell him what to do, and I thought he should figure it out without being told.

Between my practice in the morning and working on articles in the evening, I had started my next book, a treatise on the rights of refugees. Before I started my legal practice, the book writing kept my mind engaged, but now, combined with representing clients, it resulted in an often overwhelming workload. I managed to keep the household running smoothly only by planning well in advance. There was really no such institution as takeout, and the expectations of an Iranian wife include that she will cook. Leaving a sink full of dirty dishes or a hamper full of laundry is simply not an option. If I needed to travel or take a short trip for work, I arranged all the family's meals in advance. They would know to look on the top shelf of the refrigerator for that evening's cutlet, and then in the freezer for the meals labeled for the following days of the week. I even made just the right amount of fresh salad dressing and put that in the refrigerator too. I don't mean to suggest that I was a brilliant housewife or a superb cook; by Iranian standards I'm sure I could have been faulted on an array of small details and neglects. But from the beginning I had run a household that was cozier than clinically spotless, and the family was accustomed to this informality. Perhaps it was a shade fatalistic, the sometimes casual approach I took to the present. But ever since my brother-in-law Fuad's execution, when the gravity of death first touched me, I'd found preoccupation with the minutiae of daily life meaningless. If we all ultimately die, and turn to dust in the ground, should it ever truly upset us if the floor hasn't been swept quite recently enough. This didn't mean that I wasn't concerned with the details of my children's lives; it just meant that I distinguished carefully which details mattered.

To bridge my worry about spending so much time away from the house, I made a point of bringing my work home in the evening and involving the girls in what I was thinking or writing about each day. Better that they be drawn into my orbit of preoccupations, I figured, than wonder why I was so absorbed in things beyond them. I suppose deep down I hoped they would inherit my beliefs, my sensitivity to injustice, and my compulsion to push the boundaries.

The night the voting results came in for the 1996 parliamentary elections, I gathered my daughters around me on the sofa and narrated to them. Sometimes I tried to tell them about my work, to make abstract concepts such as women's rights come alive through the characters who passed through their lives. They knew, for example, that my friend Shahla Sherkat had four years ago started a women's publication called *Zanan*. It was Shahla who'd first called to tell me about Leila's case and asked whether I could offer her family legal advice. In a way, my daughters could trace the evolution in women's roles through my life and the lives of those they knew as close family friends. Before 1992, I couldn't even get a permit to work as an attorney. Shahla directed a government-owned weekly aimed at conservative, religious women. The same year I secured a license and began taking on cases, Shahla started up *Zanan*, which at first tentatively and then more forcefully took up the issues that a broader spectrum of women in Iran faced each day. Sometimes she referred cases to me; sometimes I wrote articles for her magazine.

Our budding activism was premised on a few basic facts: we lived under an Islamic Republic that was neither going anywhere nor inclined to recast its governing ethos as secular; the legal system was underpinned by Islamic law; and every facet of a woman's place in society—from access to birth control to divorce rights to compulsory veiling—was determined by interpretations of the Koran.

If we wanted to make a tangible difference in the lives of the women around us and in the lives of people like Leila and her family, we had no choice but to advocate for female equality in an Islamic framework. In this, our personal sensibilities and political worldview were wholly irrelevant. It so happened that I believed in the secular separation of religion and government because, fundamentally, Islam, like any religion, is subject to interpretation. It can be interpreted to oppress women or interpreted to liberate them. In an ideal world, I would choose not to be vulnerable to the caprice of interpretation, because the ambiguity of theological debates spirals back to the seventh century; there will never be a definitive resolution, as that is the nature and spirit of Islamic interpretation, a debate that will grow and evolve with the ages but never be resolved. I am a lawyer by training, and know only too well the permanent limitations of trying to enshrine inalienable rights in sources that lack fixed terms and definitions. But I am also a citizen of the Islamic Republic, and I know the futility of approaching the question any other way. My objective is not to vent my own political sensibilities but to push for a law that would save a family like Leila's from becoming homeless in their quest to finance the executions of their daughter's convicted murderers. If I'm forced to ferret through musty books of Islamic jurisprudence and rely on sources that stress the egalitarian ethics of Islam, then so be it. Is it harder this way? Of course it is. But is there an alternative battlefield? Desperate wishing aside, I cannot see one.

One summer morning in 1997, as I leafed through a newspaper in my office, I came across a story about a battered child who had died in a local hospital after suffering repeated blows to the head. The photo that ran with the story showed a bent little girl with thin limbs covered in cigarette burns. The photo was so painful to look at that I quickly folded it over and read on. The little girl was named Arian

Golshani. After her parents' divorce, the court granted custody of Arian to her father, a brutal man with a police record for fraud and drug addiction. According to the neighbors, the father kept Arian in dungeonlike conditions. The nine-year-old weighed only thirty-three pounds, her arms had been broken several times and plastered with makeshift casts at home, and after her schoolteacher called her father to inquire about the cigarette burn marks all over her body, she was kept home from school for months. Arian's mother went to the court and pleaded for custody; she explained her daughter's condition, explained that her ex-husband was guilty of horrific abuse. The court impassively declined to grant her custody.

All morning, the image of that scarred child remained etched in my mind. Something must be done, I felt, but what? A couple of hours later, the phone rang. A photographer friend had also seen Arian's photo in the newspaper. "Shirin, we must do something," she said. "I know, let me think," I replied. That afternoon, we convened a meeting with a few friends from a children's rights society and conferred over little cups of Turkish coffee. In the end, we devised a stealthy plan: we would arrange a ceremony ostensibly to mourn her death, but we would also use it as an occasion to protest the civil code that was its cause. We reserved space at a large mosque in central Tehran, Al-Ghadir, and took out ads in the newspaper announcing the death of Arian Golshani and the funeral ceremony in her honor. I asked Javad's uncle, a cleric, to speak about child abuse and to tell the story of her short, brutal life.

The Islamic Revolution had anointed the Muslim family the centerpiece of its ideology of nation. The revolutionaries envisioned the domesticated Muslim mother, confined to the house and caring for her multiplying brood, as key to the restoration of traditional and authentic values. Yet it seemed in no way contradictory to them to then institute a family law that automatically tore children away from mothers in the event of divorce, or made polygamy as convenient as a second mortgage. The question of child custody had weighed heavy on my own mind for years, for my older sister had long felt bound to her failing marriage partly out of fear of losing her children. It numbered among the most destructive of the system's legal codes, and articles and public outcry against the custody law had grown louder with each passing year.

On the day of the ceremony, in the fall of 1997, we lined the funeral hall with flowers and set a small table with plump dates at the entrance. Shortly before the ceremony started, several women walked through the mosque with dazed expressions, their tears flowing. They were Arian's mother and aunts. "I didn't know my daughter had so many friends," her mother said in a strangled voice, searching my face in confusion. "If so, why did she die alone?" I swallowed hard and gently led her to a seat in the front.

Javad's uncle was a gifted orator, and his speech moved the audience from the beginning. Toward the middle, a man named Alavi walked up to him holding the hand of a small child. "Here is another Arian," he said, and he recounted the child's story, his custody granted to his father but the boy desperately wishing to live with his mother. Mr. Alavi lifted the child high into the air and declared to the audience, "People, do something for these children!"

Suddenly the atmosphere grew very charged, and everyone began crying. I strode up to the microphone in the women's section and said, "Today we are here to defend the rights of other Arians. We must reform the law that led to her death." People began shouting slogans, and we asked them to disperse the flowers on the streets on their way out. The whole hall moved toward the doors at once, chanting, "The law must be reformed!" and plucking the petals from their stems.

Within half an hour, the busy streets surrounding the mosque were strewn with white petals, and the taxi drivers and commuters crawling through traffic paused to look at the mosque. Newspapers covered the story, and universities began holding seminars on child abuse. Suddenly, women's custody rights were at the center of a self-generated campaign of public awareness. My office phone, which had begun ringing more frequently ever since Leila's case, now pretty much rang incessantly. And not simply with potential clients but with journalists and international human rights monitors who needed an Iranian interlocutor on the ground to explain how the system worked and how women—not yet organized in those days—were working to change its ways.

When the trial began, I represented Arian's mother and charged the girl's father and stepbrother with torture and murder, respectively. Reporters, including broadcast journalists, crowded the courtroom, and as soon as the trial started the second row whipped out a banner reading, THE PRICE OF ARIAN'S DEATH IS A CHANGE IN THE LAWS IN FAVOR OF IRANIAN CHILDREN. Because the case had become so sensitive, the head of the branch court, a cleric, presided.

My opening statement didn't require much embellishment; the tragedy of Arian's case spoke for itself. I told the court of how she grew weak, malnourished, and disoriented after weeks of torture, how she had started to touch herself, and when her stepbrother found her with her hands between her legs, he kicked her violently, sending her tiny body flying across the floor. I described how her head cracked against the wall, sustaining the concussion that within hours killed her. I made sure to linger on the laws themselves, not simply Arian's case. I paced back and forth, my low heels clicking against the floor of the courtroom, essentially putting the law—rather than these particular defendants—on trial.

When I finished, the head of the branch court took the microphone from me. "Islam," he began ponderously, "is a religion of equality, but the Koran stipulates that a woman's inheritance is half that of a man."

How irrelevant! We were not even discussing inheritance. It was a pretext to accuse me of defaming religion.

I asked the judge permission to speak. "I am not criticizing Islam," I declared flatly. "May the tongue of anyone who does be cut.

I am criticizing a law that has been passed by the Iranian parliament. Is it fair," I asked, turning toward the court, "for a child to be abused by her father so cruelly, and for the court to deny her mother custody? Is it fair to expect a mother whose child has just been killed to pay for the execution of justice?"

"Don't worry," said the judge, assuring me that the blood money would be taken from the public treasury.

"But we don't want our taxes to go to murderers!" I said, exasperated.

The judge sentenced Arian's stepbrother to death, and her father and stepmother to one year in prison. Arian's mother eventually consented to stay the stepbrother's execution. I admired her for her compassion, as the stepbrother had been a child of the father's second marriage, and he himself had been taken from his mother after their divorce. His abuse was monstrous, but he was also a victim of the same system.

The trial's end attracted worldwide attention. CNN correspondent Christiane Amanpour interviewed me with Arian's mother, and as I watched her distraught face at home on the television, I felt heartened for a moment: though Arian's death had been senseless, at least her legacy served enormous purpose. Perhaps the Islamic Republic resisted accountability to its citizens, but it wished with each passing year to shed its pariah status in the global community. Slowly, it grew more aware that a nation on uneven footing with the West could not afford to trample its citizens' rights.

When I watched that broadcast, aware that it was being beamed around the world, I also realized for the first time that I had become what you might call famous. Prominence is something that accrues gradually. You work and speak, write articles and lecture, meet with clients and defend them, day after day, night after night, and then you wake up one day and notice that there is a long trail behind you that constitutes a reputation. That's how it happened for me, anyway. How unimportant it was to me as a person, but how useful it became to my work. It meant journalists would listen if I approached them with a case and would help publicize it both inside the country and abroad. It meant that human rights observers around the world knew and trusted me, and launched swift appeals for urgent cases I brought to their attention. It meant there was now a face and a name attached to the abstract term "human rights" in Iran, and that finally millions of women who could not articulate their frustrations and desires had someone to speak on their behalf. I would never assume such a role for myself, but in the Islamic Republic, we have a problem with representation. Our diplomats around the world are, naturally, loyal to the regime, and the regime's credibility is not such that it reflects the true opinions of the people. The responsibility falls, then, on unofficial ambassadors to relate Iranians' perceptions and hopes to the world.

Between my ever-growing reputation and the world's curiosity about how women fared in a society like Iran's, it seemed more possible each year to make the system pay an international price for its refusal to reform its laws at home.

CHAPTER EIGHT

Terror and the Republic

ONLY AFTER THE BUS DRIVER ABANDONED THE MOVING coach for the second time did Fereshteh Sari realize that he was trying to kill them. Around twenty Iranian novelists and poets were traveling to Armenia for a literary conference, and they had chartered a passenger bus to drive them through the winding mountains of northern Iran, wooded by oaks and wild pear and walnut trees, to the country's western province. When my friend Fereshteh had dropped by my house for tea the day before leaving, she'd described the trip as a much-anticipated chance to see the antique cobblestones of the capital and to indulge in long, evening conversations with her fellow writers.

At about two in the morning, with most of the writers dozing in their seats, the driver stopped the bus at the side of the road and hopped out. One of the writers up front noticed that the hand brake had not been pulled, and he called out to the driver, assuming he'd gotten sleepy and needed a quick break. The driver boarded the bus, started it back up, and pulled out onto the road, navigating the narrow two lanes that snaked between the towering peaks, guided by moonlight. A sharp acceleration jolted most of the writers awake. They watched in terror as the bus hurtled toward a cliff edge. As it neared the precipice, the driver flung his door open and jumped out. A writer up front hurled himself into the driver's seat and jammed on the brakes, pulling the bus to a screeching stop. They stared out into the dark abyss beyond the mountain's edge, the bus unsteady beneath them. One of the tires had nearly gone over, and the nose of the bus hung over the edge. One by one, the writers filed out.

They gathered in shock on the dirt on the side of the Heyran Pass and stared at one another mutely. Not long after, a security officer arrived and drove them to a small town on the lush green plain near the Caspian Sea for interrogation. The interrogator warned them to discuss the event with no one, then allowed them to return to Tehran. Fereshteh recounted the story to me in my living room the day she returned. I felt a tremor of fear in my stomach. Throughout the early and mid-nineties, the regime hunted its opponents across Europe, dispatching assassins to kill elderly shah-era officials, political activists, and, in one case, a popular singer with critical views. It was August 1996, and we could no longer pretend that the campaign of terror only struck abroad. Two days before Fereshteh had left for Armenia, another friend, the poet Simin Behbahani, had told me that a dinner she'd attended at the home of a German diplomat had been raided, and that she and two other writers had been detained overnight. The previous fall, a translator in Isfahan had been killed, his body left lying in the street. Another writer, Ghafar Hosseini, died of a suspicious heart attack in his home two months later.

Many of the writers belonged to the Writers Association of Iran, a collection of novelists, translators, poets, and intellectuals that gathered each month to discuss literature, censorship, and how to defend freedom of expression in the country. I had joined the association myself, and after the Armenia bus trip and the mysterious disappearances, we grew convinced that a dark, stealthy wave of terror had been initiated against us. It was a harrowing time. All of us imagined that our phones were tapped and our movements followed. Too many strange coincidences—meetings raided at precisely opportune moments, unfamiliar new faces surfacing in the group—signaled that we were being watched at all times.

Every time I had to attend one of our meetings, I took the new precaution we all deemed necessary. We met in different parts of Tehran, first near a major bookstore in Palestine Square, later at the Naderi Café, a worn old downtown coffeehouse with vaulted ceilings overlooking a garden, famed as a gathering hole for writers and intellectuals earlier in the century. I changed taxis several times en route. In Iran, taxis also operate like small buses, servicing particular routes, so I would hail a passenger taxi, switch at a major intersection to a private one, then get out again several blocks away and jump in another. It was no secret who we were. We had signed our names to protest letters in the past, to make clear to the government that our work as intellectuals was not political. Back in 1994, the same year a prominent literary critic died mysteriously in government custody, 134 writers had signed an open letter to the system protesting censorship and demanding freedom of expression and association. I had signed that letter too. After its publication, a number of the signatories were killed or disappeared. Now it seemed that a faceless death squad was coming after us. Picking us off one by one.

*I*n the dark days that followed, it was impossible not to compare the repression we were facing with what activists endured under the shah's regime, in its prisons and at the hands of the SAVAK, its secret police. But this campaign of intimidation was wholly different from how the shah had dealt with his opponents. The SAVAK operated like a classic security arm of an autocracy; it homed in on very specific targets, political activists openly opposing the shah's regime, and tried to break them with traditional devices of physical torture: electric shock, nail extraction.

The techniques the Islamic Republic employed departed from the SAVAK style of repression, as well as from that of its own wave of terror in the early years of the revolution. It marked a new phase in the regime's political evolution, a change that reflected a more modern concern for the sensibilities of the international community. First of all, the intelligence apparatus of the Islamic Republic reached far and wide, and did not draw the line at dissidents; its mandate included the targeting of translators of French literature as well as organized political activists calling for a secular government.

In the early 1990s, after the war, human rights rapporteurs and watchdog groups started documenting the waves of executions and the wanton abuses of human rights the regime perpetrated. The mass MKO executions of 1988, in which Fuad, along with thousands of others, had been killed, had blackened the reputation of a system trying to integrate back into the international community so that it could rebuild itself after war and tend its burgeoning population. It was around the time of the bus incident that we noticed how the style of crackdown was changing.

The system no longer felt comfortable announcing to the world, in newspapers filled with photos of shot corpses, We kill our opposition. To evade condemnation and outcry by the international community, officials concluded that trials and executions needed to be handled differently. In the past, they held trials in which they themselves had gathered the evidence, in which there was no lawyer, trials that were held behind closed doors—swift, secret kangaroo trials that resulted in death sentences. In a justice system where the roles of prosecutor, judge, and interrogator bled into one, swift sentences were easier to hand down. Since the prisoners usually didn't mount a defense, the officials' thinking went, and since we have so much evidence anyway, why even hold a trial? Why don't we just present the file to a couple of clerics and get their permission for a death warrant? This way, the theological requirements were satisfied, and the Ministry of Intelligence could send out its death squad to execute the sentence. The assassins varied their techniques—some of their victims died in car accidents, others were shot in staged robberies; some were stabbed in the street or gunned down; one popular method was to inject a target with potassium to produce a seemingly natural heart attack. Whoever had ordered the killings must have thought this was very clever. They must have believed that it would escape the attention of the international community that every few months an Iranian writer or opposition figure would turn up dead on the side of the road, or keel over from an unexpected, fatal heart attack.

The scariest thing about those times was the caprice with which the state chose its victims. Perhaps this was precisely the mission: to terrorize the intellectual and literary circles of Tehran so thoroughly that no one would dare raise their voice in criticism. If a scholar of neoclassical Persian literature was murdered in prison, what fate might befall those who explicitly challenged the core of the system, the divine right of the ayatollahs to rule? We gathered frequently in those days, squinting into the tea leaves, trying to discern a pattern or a reason in the choice of targets.

Though the Islamic Republic worked to clean up its international reputation, its past activities dogged its efforts, and it often went into a Soviet mode of damage control that only worsened matters. In 1997, a German court ordered the arrest of Minister of Intelligence Ali Fallahian for directing the murder of Iranian-Kurdish dissidents at a Berlin restaurant in 1992. The ruling humiliated the Islamic Republic. A standing cabinet minister implicated in the Mafia-style gunning down of dissidents marred the regime's tentative efforts to moderate its image. In retaliation, the government claimed that German spies were infiltrating Iran. But who? Where? Officials selected Faraj Sarkuhi, a mild-mannered journalist and a member of the Writers Association, who had the misfortune of having a family in Germany. Faraj had also attended the raided dinner party of the German diplomat, and his detention that evening was later invoked as evidence of espionage.

Faraj drove to Tehran's Mehrabad Airport one evening for a flight to Germany and never came out. His wife reported that he never arrived, though airport records showed that his passport had been stamped for exit. We were all confused, and quite nervous for him. A month later, he showed up again at Mehrabad, with a wild story of having fled to Tajikistan and Georgia after fighting with his wife in Germany. He said nothing of having been detained, and we remained stupefied. In keeping with the film-noir atmosphere of those times, a photocopied letter surfaced in the bookstores of Tehran, in which Faraj detailed his kidnapping at the airport and the account of his farcical reemergence there. The letter described how his interrogators in prison forced him to "confess" on camera to spying for Germany, and to affairs with women. "I was arrested, and I have no doubt that I will soon be killed," he wrote. And, indeed, two weeks later he was arrested again.

One afternoon, Faraj's mother came to visit me in my office. The hesitant, elderly woman sat in a chair opposite me, asked if I would take on Faraj's case, then promptly burst into tears. Faraj had spent time in the shah's prisons, she said, inconsolable. Was that not enough? In between tearful accounts of his prison days under the shah, it became clear that money was running short. I wanted to help her without wounding her pride. "Mrs. Sarkuhi," I said, "Faraj has left some money with me. Why don't you let me give it to you?" Of course he had done no such thing, but I thought her pride might allow her to take some help from me if I offered it in this manner. She was brave and sweet and, seeing through my ruse, refused to take any money.

Armed with her power of attorney, I set about my investigation, but I didn't know where to start. I decided to begin with the Islamic Human Rights Commission, a supposed nongovernmental organization (NGO) that was housed in a government building and headed by the chief of the judiciary. Some NGO. Their main contribution to defending Faraj's human rights was to inform me that he had drafted a letter in prison rejecting my counsel. I pointed out that the letter was dated *before* his mother had even asked me to represent him. To no avail. They didn't allow me to defend Faraj, so I made my case to the press when his verdict was announced. I argued that according to the constitution, political crimes must be tried in an open court, and because Faraj was accused of propagating lies to undermine the state, his closed trial was therefore illegal. Eventually, the court appointed a lawyer for Faraj; he spent a year in solitary confinement, and, thankfully, came out alive. I think the photocopied letter might have saved him.

When he was released from prison, Faraj invited me to dinner at Sorrento, a restaurant on Vali Asr, the crowded, sycamore-lined central boulevard that runs through Tehran. We settled into the maroon vinyl booths, and he told me that he wanted to leave the country but feared being arrested again should he apply for a passport. "Don't worry," I reassured him, "I'll go with you." The next day we drove to the passport office in Tehran's bustling downtown, a two-story building that Faraj entered with nervous eyes. He obtained a passport, left Iran for Germany, and never returned.

Faraj's case taught us much about how the system would go about dealing with its perceived opposition. Those arrested, whether on charges of espionage or of plotting to overthrow the regime, typically faced sophisticated methods of torture and intimidation that did not leave telltale marks on the body, yet efficiently brutalized the detained into making videotaped confessions that would later be aired on state television. Sleep deprivation, mock executions, foot lashings, mind games played with fake newspapers that told of mass arrests or coups d'état, solitary confinement in cells the size of fox-holes—these methods replaced the cruder physical torture employed by the SAVAK. Nail extraction, hot grills, and electrical cattle prods were abandoned, and often, after a detained person emerged from prison, they bore few scars or little physical evidence of their interrogation. Though they had typically lost thirty pounds, could not sleep through the night, and had a permanently hollow look in their eyes, the system could parade them before the world and claim it had not resorted to physical torture.

*I*t was at once a gothic horror story, with a dark, chilling villain, and a mystery tale, complete with bungling investigators, a muckraking journalist who spun the plot with coded names like "Eminence Grise," and a setting that he called a "dark house of ghosts." It resulted in a serious rift in the system, between the government of the sitting reformist president, Mohammad Khatami, and his still powerful predecessor, Akbar Hashemi Rafsanjani.

On the evening of November 22, 1998, the evening bulletin on the Persian-language radio station broke for an urgent piece of news. Dariush and Parvaneh Forouhar, dissident intellectuals, had been murdered in their Tehran home. The assassins had stabbed the elderly couple repeatedly, then escaped into the night. I was on a brief visit to the United States at the time and considered postponing my return to Tehran. In the end, I went back, for the killings were so singularly brutal that I did not imagine more could follow.

Three nights later, the news reported that the body of Majid Sharif, a translator who had left his home for a jog the previous week and never returned, had been found at the Tehran coroner's office. Ten days after that, the writer Mohammad Mokhtari disappeared while buying lightbulbs on Jordan Boulevard, in north Tehran. A few days later, his suffocated body turned up in south Tehran. That same evening, Mohammad Jafar Pouyandeh, another writer, disappeared; his body surfaced at the coroner's office on December 13, 1998.

Supreme Leader Ayatollah Ali Khamenei expressed shock at the murders during that week's Friday prayers. President Khatami called them "disgusting acts" aimed at bringing down the Islamic system. He ordered a committee to investigate the serial murders. I was cautiously pleased to hear the president's announcement, but since the state for years had declined accountability for its extrajudicial violence, I reserved judgment.

On January 6, 1999, a friend called me and said, "You will never believe what has happened." That day, the Ministry of Intelligence had issued a statement that said, "Unfortunately a number of irresponsible, misled, and maverick colleagues of ours ... have perpetrated these criminal acts." It was the first time in the history of the Islamic Republic that the government had accepted responsibility for the killing of a critic. About a month later, the minister of intelligence, Ghorbanali Dorri-Najafabadi, resigned. The story only grew.

A couple of months later, Parastou Forouhar, the daughter of the slain couple, sought me out and asked if I would legally represent her family. I agreed. We spent long hours together, piecing together information from the police, the neighbors, and the household servant, trying to figure out exactly what had transpired that fateful night of her parents' killing.

*I*n the days leading up to their murders, Dariush and Parvaneh Forouhar lived in constant fear of death. They were both long-standing and outspoken critics of the regime, Dariush in particular. He was the leader of the Iran Nation Party (Hezb-e Mellat-e Iran), the group dating its origins to the party of the deposed prime minister Mohammad Mossadegh, and had spent years in prison under the shah's regime for his activism. He supported the revolution and became the Islamic Republic's first minister of labor, but like many secular nationalists who opposed the Islamic radicalism that grew out of the revolution, he stepped down and returned to the familiar role of opposition. Though the Forouhars grew more explicit in their opposition to the Islamic regime over time, criticizing the republic's constitution and its autocratic delegation of power to the supreme leader, their organization posed no real threat to the government. Its followers included aging intellectuals and scholars, and a smattering of young college students.

Though they were no more dangerous to the Islamic regime than a storm of down feathers, the Ministry of Intelligence harassed the Forouhars day in and day out for years. Their two children were interrogated so many times that they eventually moved to Germany. Their every conversation was recorded. They installed bars on their windows, and Dariush kept a bag ready with toiletries should he be taken away to prison.

Sometime after eleven P.M. on that cool November evening, as Dariush was entertaining friends in his study, one of his guests leaped up and tied his body to a chair. The assassins stabbed him eleven times, turned his body toward Mecca, and left the blood to collect in a pool around him. Parvaneh was upstairs getting ready for bed. She was stabbed twenty-four times. Afterward both their bodies were hacked to pieces. Friends found them the next day, when they went over and saw the front door open, their pet dog drugged.

The carpets, furniture, and bedsheets were caked with dried blood. After the investigators combed through the house, several items went missing: a notebook of Parvaneh's poetry; Dariush's diary, where he had recorded his thoughts on the concept of *velayat-e faqih*, Ayatollah Khomeini's doctrine of absolute rule by the clergy; the treasured correspondence between Dariush and his hero, Prime Minister Mossadegh.

Before the case even went to trial, it fell apart. A faction within the state, it appeared, was as determined to cover up the scandal as the president was to unearth it. Though President Khatami was democratically minded at heart and had promised Iranians to make their country more lawful, he quickly found that in the Islamic Republic the executive branch wielded little power. A deputy minister of intelligence with close ties to senior officials, Saeed Emami, was named the lead suspect. Not long after he was implicated and detained in the case, he allegedly committed suicide in prison by swallowing a bottle of hair-removal cream. When Emami died, so did any real chance of prosecuting senior regime officials for their role in ordering the killings. It was clear that Emami, a mid-ranking official with ties to the security apparatus, was much more than just a ringleader of a death cell. His friends reported that he belonged to a notorious gang of hard-core religious extremists who believed that the enemies of Islam should be killed. Shadowy reports of this gang and its activities were whispered from mouth to mouth in Tehran. If there was a cabal within the apparatus of state with a mission to liquidate opponents and create a climate of terror that discouraged dissent, few doubted that Saeed Emami was its heart.

When I read the stories of his suicide in the papers, I grew curious. "Ladies, please go buy every brand of hair-removal cream available," I instructed my staff. Every single one of the bottles they brought back was labeled "no arsenic." It seemed impossible to commit suicide with any over-the-counter depilatory on the Iranian market. I wondered if perhaps the suicide story was a sham, and that Emami was actually alive. The only way to find out was to attend the ceremonies commemorating his death, to see whether his relatives' tears were real or staged.

On a warm afternoon in June 1999, I dragged my sister along to the ceremonies at a Tehran mosque. It was so hot inside that I immediately gulped down two glasses of orange *sharbat*. "Now that he's dead," I whispered to her, "at least the drinks are on him." We giggled behind our black chadors, and once I surveyed the room, I had to again fight back a smile. The crowd was full of familiar faces, other journalists and activists peering around as suspiciously as I was, to see whether the wails of grief were genuine or fake. Few who followed such matters closely found the convenient prison suicide of the lead suspect in the case terribly convincing. Saeed Emami's wife and sister bawled noisily in the front row, and a stout woman who looked like an undercover policewoman constantly shushed them quiet. His sister, nearly hysterical, kept screaming, "*Haj* Saeed, I wish I could tell all." After the ceremony was over, my sister tugged at my arm to leave, but I walked over to Mrs. Emami and offered her my condolences. I took one look at her red-rimmed eyes, felt her unsteady hand in mine, and knew that her husband was dead.

Around roughly this same time, a series of investigative articles ran in the popular newspaper *Sobh-e Emrouz,* unraveling the scandal for the public. The author, an investigative journalist named Akbar Ganji, relied on sources within the country's intelligence apparatus to outline the secret plan enacted by the state to eliminate its critics. Ganji's journalism mesmerized Iranians, who stood in line each morning at the newspaper kiosks, eager to follow the latest twists in the narrative. Though Ganji used coded nicknames to describe the senior clerics who had issued the fatwas, or Islamic decrees, that served as death sentences, everyone knew which officials he was referring to.

In the summer of 1999, as Ganji continued to wage his aggressive journalism, the judiciary finally ceded to our requests to gain access to the files. At the same time, the system sought to undermine our investigation. The judiciary chief ordered a closed-door trial and imposed a gag order on the attorneys, barring them from speaking to the press. Several ranking officials declared that the suspects, including the now deceased Saeed Emami, had acted under orders from the Islamic Republic's "foreign enemies" to taint the system's international reputation. A videotape of Saeed Emami's wife confessing to this (a technique Ganji dubbed the "self-inflicted interview") was leaked to the media. During her detainment, when the tape was made, she was tortured so badly that one of her kidneys failed.

In the ten days that I and the other lawyers of the victims' families were permitted to read the files, we were not allowed to make any photocopies, even though the dossier ran to thousands of pages. There were dates missing throughout, and a glaring absence of substantive information, such as transcripts of the lead suspect's interrogation. Though much of what was directly relevant to the investigation was missing from the files, we did find numerous arresting details that illuminated the history of the extrajudicial killings. It was in reading these files that I first encountered my own name, and discovered that the same death squad had intended to kill me.

For a long time, I never mentioned this directly to anyone in the government. A couple of years later, an official stopped by my office and requested that I speak at a conference the government was organizing in Europe on the terrorist activities of the Mojahedin-e Khalgh. "If you want me to come talk about MKO terrorism," I told him, "then I will also need to talk about how all of you, the government, tried to kill me. Is that all right?" He said nothing. "I presume you won't consider me a very effective speaker," I concluded. Sometimes the psychology of the Islamic regime baffled me, how it could with one hand seek the aid of a person the other hand sought to kill.

In the summer of 1999, the trial petered to a disappointing end. Two of the suspects were sentenced to life imprisonment, the actual assassins to death, and all the others received short prison terms. The supreme court later overturned some of the verdicts, but the lawyers of the families never learned of its final decision, since the proceedings were kept confidential, on grounds of national security. No senior official ever faced prosecution, and the presiding intelligence minister at the time of the killings was later promoted to an extremely senior position in the judiciary. Saeed Emami's direct supervisor in the Ministry of Intelligence later ran for president. You might think that because no death sentence was ever carried out, because the implicated senior officials carried on their political careers, the case of the serial killings left only a fleeting legacy in the Islamic Republic.

But after the trial concluded, widows and relatives of other murdered dissidents began arriving at my office regularly. The code of silence, instilled by fear of the ministry and belief in its impregnability, had been broken. The Islamic Republic learned that it was a house divided: the rift in the regime helped produce the scandal; the scandal in turn widened the rift between the regime and the people. Since that summer, the Ministry of Intelligence has ceased ordering the execution of dissidents and intellectuals.

My own experience with the case is hard to appraise. It was the first time in my life that I confronted the possibility of my own death directly, and my abstract worry forever after turned to real fear. When I planned vacations, I would find myself looking at the map and wondering, Hmm, would it be easier for me to be assassinated here or there? I have been commended for not giving up, even after finding out that I was also a target. But by then the case had taken on a dimension larger than me, larger than the killings themselves, larger than any of us could ever have imagined.

It was not one of the most successful trials of my life, as it never produced reform in a law, or even a worthy conviction. But it pulled back the curtains on what Ganji described as the "dark house of ghosts," a shadowy country where assassins took their victims in the night and slunk off, unaccountable. It made killing less cheap, and less easy. It forced the Islamic Republic to check its excess, to discard extrajudicial killings, as it had discarded mass executions a decade prior. If the words did not stick so in my throat, I would call it an evolution.

CHAPTER NINE

An Experiment in Hope

ON MAY 23, 1997, TWENTY-TWO MILLION IRANIANS VOTED
to give the Islamic Republic a second chance. Under
cheery spring skies with scarcely a hint of clouds, they
lined the streets of Tehran, and other cities around the
country, to cast their votes for a little-known man
named Mohammad Khatami, who at that moment
perhaps symbolized more the opposite of what Iranians knew they did *not* want than what they did. It was
the first time in recent memory that a dark-horse candidate had challenged an establishment politician, and
the unexpected contest roused people's hope that with
Khatami's election, their lives might tangibly improve.

Unlike the favored candidate, he did not belong to
the revolutionary political elite, and his rhetoric lacked
the ubiquitous references to enemy and martyr, "Great
Satan" and "Zionist Enemy." He promised to transform Iran into an Islamic democracy, a country governed by the rule of law, on better terms with its
neighbors and the world. This election, like so many of
its predecessors, was not a pure exercise of democracy,
for many candidates—those deemed "outsiders," from
religious nationalists to secularists—were not allowed

to run. But the "insiders" on the ballot differed sufficiently for the race to be competitive, and people still felt that by voting they could play some role in determining the nation's direction. Election Day, the second of Khordad in the Iranian calendar, fell on a Friday, and the lines around the schools and mosques where people voted extended all the way down city blocks.

It was the first presidential election for Negar, my eldest daughter, and my youngest laced up her shoes too, to come watch us vote. We walked to our local polling station, a nearby school, and joined all the young and old people standing in line, chatting with the familiarity of relatives. I didn't see a single woman wearing a chador, and the warmth and high spirits of the people in line reminded me of the early moments of the revolution, when for a few fleeting days everyone called each other "brother" and "sister," carried each other's groceries, and generally behaved as a collective family. That was before the mercenary culture of the revolutionary years set in and people began behaving dysfunctionally, second-guessing each other's motives, preemptively lying and cheating so as not to be cheated, clanking doors in the faces of the elderly. "Khatami is not like the rest of them," I remember a woman in line saying. "He actually wants to help us."

When we arrived at my mother's house for Friday lunch, she emerged from the kitchen with her hands on her hips. "Why didn't you take me with you?" she demanded. "Because it was crowded," I said, "and you couldn't have stood in line for a whole hour." "Fine," she sighed, "but then you shall have to take me in the afternoon." At around six, before the evening voters turned out in droves, we found a small polling station with a shortish line. It was the first time since the 1979 revolution that my mother, now eighty years old, had voted. The polling staff saw her waiting and clucked around her until she agreed to sit in a folding metal chair, while I held her place in line. A few other older ladies who had already cast their votes gathered around her, and from their circle snatches of conversation—"Things have gotten so awful," "*Inshallah*, Khatami can do something for us"—floated back to me. When her turn came, I called her up and began filling out her ballot. But she grabbed my wrist, saying, "Please, Shirin *jan*, I have to do it myself." As we walked away, she told me, "I wish your father was still alive." She said this very rarely. It was her way of saying, I'm happy right now.

She didn't leave the house much in those days, so I figured I should take advantage of our outing and stop for ice cream. "Shirin, do not order me an ice-cream sandwich," she said. "It's going to drip on me." At eighty she was more fastidious than ever. I got her little scoops of fresh vanilla ice cream in a cup, and myself the wafer sandwich. Mine, of course, dripped, and she just shook her head. Javad came home late for dinner that night, and explained that he had been out at our small orchard on the outskirts of Tehran and had ended up ferrying the workers back and forth to the village polling station.

Delirious, spontaneous joy—of the sort, please remember, that had not been on display in the streets of Tehran in over two decades—swept the neighborhoods of the city when the radio began reporting Khatami's lead. I was out in the street, and people hurtled past me on all sides, hugging one another and chattering amid peals of congratulations. Outside the local pastry shop, the baker's apprentice stood in the street handing out sweets to passersby.

The victory of Mohammad Khatami took everyone, from our neighborhood to the upper echelons of the clerical establishment, by utter surprise. A former culture minister with a reputation for bookishness, he lacked all the usual credentials by which clerics rise to power in the Islamic Republic: a revolutionary record, muscular ties to power-broker ayatollahs. In nearly every way—except, of course, the clerical turban on his head and his loyalty to the revolution—he departed from everything we had become accustomed to in our post-1979 leaders. A genuine, shining smile always played on his lips, as opposed to the usual flat grimace. He wore elegant, finely woven robes in hues of chocolate and pear instead of the wrinkled, mud-colored robes common among clerics. On his feet, he wore polished leather loafers, instead of the leather sandals or, worse, plastic flip-flops that became standard footwear after the revolution. For years, the images of our leaders that were televised into our living rooms showed them holding meetings cross-legged on the floor, wearing unkempt robes and often unkempt beards. The appeal of Khatami's refinement did not mean that Iranians no longer cared about pop-ulism, or that a large segment of the population were less poor. It meant that in the interim twenty years, they had come to despise clerical hypocrisy.

For they knew very well that the revolutionaries who had dis-placed the shah's cronies from the seats of power and from the wooded villas of north Tehran had slipped into their places. The vast oil reserves from which the shah had derived his wealth provided those close to the new system with a similar opportunity for self-enrichment. In two decades, a new rich and revolutionary elite had emerged from among the populist radicals of 1979, who that year had proclaimed that Islam would solve all of Iran's economic problems; their grandiose promises of free cars and free food had, of course, not been delivered. Real per capita income declined after the revolution, and the majority of Iranians had to work two or more jobs just to make ends meet. Meanwhile, the clerics in power established them-selves and their families in luxurious homes in the fresh-aired upper reaches of north Tehran. They drove, or were chauffeured in, expen-sive foreign cars that screamed "powerful revolutionary politician" amid the sea of decaying, sputtering old Iranian Paykans that filled the city's thoroughfares.

The rampant corruption alienated the vast majority of Iranians, who could scarcely conduct even the most basic transactions in their lives without bribery or connections. The clerics and their cronies did not fly to Europe for lunch as the shah's ministers had, but their raiding of the state's coffers was noticed by everyone. The shop assistant in the Tehran bazaar who had driven Ayatollah Khomeini's car upon his return from exile, for example, was transformed into one of the wealthiest men in all Iran. Prominent politicians became notorious for using their regime connections to secure monopolies on lucrative imports and exports.

But the regime clung to its revolutionary ideology in the face of this spiraling corruption and watched its legitimacy steadily erode. Billboards and murals of grim-faced war martyrs and portraits of founding clerics hung across the city, whose every other street was renamed for a martyr. The murals cried DEATH TO AMERICA and embraced the cult of martyrdom that grew out of the Iran-Iraq War, and many celebrated Iran's support for militant groups in distant places such as Lebanon and Palestine. Often the artwork took on a ghoulish and kitschy aesthetic, with a skull for the head of the Statue of Liberty, or a portrait of a mother cradling a baby dressed up as a suicide bomber. The dogmatism of these images pervaded the public space in Iran and fed the indignation of ordinary Iranians who felt that the clerics became wealthier each day, while preaching of sacrifice, struggle, and revolutionary Islam from the pulpit during Friday prayers.

Khatami stepped onto the stage with this as his backdrop, and charmed the nation. He abandoned the stale rhetoric about enemies and foreign plots, instead invoking the rule of law and democracy in his speeches. Conversant in philosophers from Plato to Alexis de Tocqueville, he held young people and women in particular spellbound with his respectful, heartfelt references to their importance in Iranian society. What made Khatami different was precisely what made him useful. The Islamic Republic badly needed to restore its credibility in the eyes of the disillusioned younger generation. With his youthful appeal and his deep allegiance to the Islamic system, Khatami was the ideal way to loosen up Iran without weakening the regime.

His landslide victory, a staggering 70 percent of the vote, amounted to an unequivocal popular mandate for change. But the dreamy expectations in line around me on Election Day unsettled me. People didn't seem to want reform so much as a whole new Iran, and in four years, please, thank you very much. People wanted all the laws that discriminated against women to be wiped from the books. They wanted financial corruption abolished. They imagined that overnight the justice system would become independent. They thought that those who had executed their relatives in the last two decades, those who had ordered the firing squads to shoot, would finally be tried. The longing and expectation ran so deep that, frankly, I was frightened.

People's yearnings have overtaken their realism, I thought. Don't they know what circumscribed powers our constitution affords a president? Are they not aware of the intricate legal framework by which a handful of unelected clerical officials can unravel and determine policy, so as to render a president nearly irrelevant? There was no way Khatami could meet all these expectations. Unfortunately, Iranians are at heart hero worshippers. Whether it is the Rostam of our ancient epic poem the *Shahnameh* (The Book of Kings), or Imam Hossein, the martyr-saint of Shiism, they cling to the notion that one lofty, iconic figure can sweep through their lives, slay their enemies, and turn their world around. Perhaps other cultures also believe in heroes, but Iranians do so with a unique devotion. Not only do they fall in love with heroes, but they are in love with their love for them. In voting for Khatami, they believed they had done their part, and they settled back in a haze of moony adoration, waiting for him to transform Iran into the paradise of their imaginations.

For a few stretches during the years 1998 and 1999, the country experienced a flowering of open debate and freedom of the press that some optimistic souls called a Tehran spring. The optimism was perhaps not entirely unwarranted, for the practice of censorship extended far back into the reaches of Iranian history, even into the era of the modernizing shah. After the revolution, the Islamic Republic controlled the media so thoroughly that most of my friends did not even bother buying newspapers, and turned instead to Persian-language BBC and Voice of America radio for news. But Khatami changed all of that, giving his Culture Ministry free run to issue press permits for new publications, and for a brief time the media operated in an atmosphere of relative freedom and independence.

The newspapers enhanced our morning routines delightfully. I picked up five or six regularly, and sat down with a steaming cup of tea, savoring the new ritual; it was so civilizing to finally have a national conversation about where the country was headed. The newspapers also breathed life back into the public spaces. People talked about the headlines in line at the kiosks, in the back of taxicabs, and on buses. The suffocating sense that we could speak freely only in our living rooms, that the street was off-limits to our real thoughts and reflexive opinions, gradually receded. Most Iranians, especially young people, hoped that the independent press signaled a greater broadening of freedoms in Iranian society, or at least their potential. If the future suddenly seemed brighter, that's because its horizon was on the front page.

The ruling establishment's tolerance for the press's freedom did not last long. A liberalized press opened up space for political dissent, and the hard-line clerics feared that criticism would be the beginning of their undoing. Determined to hold fast to their influence, they moved to silence their critics. On the morning of July 7, 1999, the hard-line judiciary ordered the popular independent newspaper *Salaam* shut. The newspaper and its editor were charged with violating national security code for having crossed the regime's red lines. The paper had run articles linking senior officials to the killings of dozens of dissidents, in effect calling the state into account for its practice of stealthily murdering its opponents, as well as those it simply found annoying. When students around the city heard the news, they gathered at the campus of Tehran University to protest the paper's closure.

That evening, about four hundred plainclothes paramilitaries descended on a university dormitory, whispering into short-wave radios and wielding green sticks. According to students' accounts, uniformed policemen stood by and did nothing. The paramilitaries kicked down doors and smashed through the halls. They grabbed female students by the hair and set fire to rooms. They thrashed about with their batons and flung students off third-floor balconies. Several crashed down onto the pavement below, their bones crushed. One lay paralyzed. Shots must also have been fired, because students turned up at hospitals with bullet wounds. Witnesses reported that at least one student was killed, three hundred wounded, and thousands detained in the days that followed.

My family and I had been out of town that weekend, and we drove back into the city around midnight. Pulling up at a major intersection near the university, we gazed around in confusion. Contingents of police trucks rumbled past in tandem, toward a barrier erected by security forces cordoning off the whole perimeter of the campus. The news reported that there had been skirmishes at the university, but the area was so heavily blockaded by police that we didn't dare approach. Through air hung heavy with tension, the officers waved us on, as though away from a disaster scene.

The next day the unrest began in earnest, spreading to provincial cities. The true origins of what happened next are still contested in Iran. This much was clear: five days of rioting turned Tehran into a battlefield, inarguably the worst mass disturbance the system had seen in its twenty-year life span. Some scenes were straight out of the mass protests that led up to the 1979 revolution. After the second day, the rioting took on a life of its own, a destructive, violent rampage that left a gutted downtown Tehran in its wake, burned-out buses, and smashed storefronts. There were running street battles across the avenues and squares of the city, as students pelted security forces with stones, setting alight pictures of the supreme leader. The clashes grew more deadly each day; plainclothes security officers fired shots into the air to disperse students, police fired tear gas into crowds, and trucks waited to cart off students by the hundreds for detention. Police helicopters circled above central Tehran, calling on students to disperse over echoing megaphones. In pictures of those days, Tehran looks like the scene of a civil war, fought street to street. There are row after row of policemen in riot gear, facing off against a crowd of young people with extended fists, smoke and rubble all around them.

In the course of those few days, time seemed to slow. No one knew what would come next: Would tanks roll through the streets of Tehran? Might the protests swell to the millions? It felt as though the fate of the country hung in the balance.

I decided that this was the perfect opportunity to give my daughters a guided tour of an Iranian disturbance. Like young people anywhere, Iranian youth are easily seduced by the siren song of political protest. When you're young, you don't think about all that might happen, all that is encompassed in a large protest. You are not yet seasoned enough to question whether the young man standing next to you, crying bravely for the dismissal of the supreme leader, might be a paid agent sent into the crowd to incite others. You only see the shining, excited faces of those around you, you feel their bodies press up against yours as the protest surges forward, and you feel exhilarated by the rare, exhilarating sense of your own power. You are not just another Iranian teenager with sour, passive grievances at your lack of social freedom; you are a citizen, an actor, capable of turning your capital into a war zone.

Like most Iranian parents, I was worried that my daughters would be lured into marching headfirst into the murk and chaos of the protests. Wailing, worried mothers already lined the curb outside Evin Prison, holding vigil while waiting for news of their missing children. I had no wish to join them. My greatest apprehension has always been that my daughters would be used to crush me. If they were ever picked up on some pretext or another—wearing nail polish or passing by a protest—and it was discovered that they were my daughters, they would doubtlessly be treated much, much more harshly.

After lunch, I told Negar and Nargess to put on their *roopooshes,* their Islamically correct coats, and we drove down to Tehran University. The surrounding streets were eerily silent, the bookshops closed, policemen at every corner. On campus, people gathered under trees, on steps outside lecture halls, arguing heatedly. Occasionally, an activist would walk past, lugging bags of soda and food for the students. As we passed the modernist facade of a lecture hall, one of the larger groups erupted in loud, confrontational slogans.

"Please pay attention to this," I said, turning to the girls, guiding them slowly back to the group. "It is not important whether what he is chanting is true or not, whether you believe in it or not. Your decision to chant along with him is no measure of your commitment to justice or freedom or whatever lofty principle is at hand. Sometimes, radical slogans are a trap. They are shouted by infiltrators so that a group of students protesting a press crackdown can be depicted as seeking to overthrow the regime. Sometimes they are not traps at all but the frustrated stand of a brave person. But how are you to know? Your objective is to avoid being a pawn, to avoid getting dragged into trouble because you are curious, or believe you are seeing history being made."

They nodded solemnly.

After all this, what did Negar do the next day? She went straight back to campus with her friends and loitered around. After a while, fighting broke out.

I was at home when she phoned.

"Maman, can you hear me?" she asked tremulously when I picked up.

"Where on earth are you?" I exploded. "Negar, *are those gunshots I hear?*"

She and her friends had fled from the campus and taken refugee at a house across the street.

She gave me the phone number. Half an hour later, when I tried to call, the phone just rang and rang. My stomach knotted. I wanted to drive over and pick her up right then, but the streets were too chaotic. My brother lived nearby, and I asked him to walk over and find her.

"She's fine," he reported back wryly. "They're on the roof, for a better view of the clashes."

Finally, at around eleven, when the streets had calmed, I drove through the darkened center of town, past the charred police stations and the storefronts with shattered windows, to pick up Negar. I resolved to remain calm when she jumped in the car. I didn't scold her, and I kept my tone even.

"Negar *jan*," I said, "I took you to the university myself yesterday to prevent exactly this. I would like to ask you a couple of questions."

She blinked at me innocently.

"If there were men in that house and they assaulted you, what would you have done? If you had been arrested and were sitting in prison right now instead of in this car, what would you have done? If you had been shot, where would you be now? Don't ever forget: if you are ever arrested, you will be treated far worse than others because you are my daughter. They can't touch me, but they can touch you. Through you, they will try to intimidate me. It goes without saying that you should be careful at all times. But please, bear this last point in mind."

We drove home in silence, and arrived to find Javad just back from the gym, his hair still wet. When I laid eyes on him, relaxed from swimming laps, the true difference between a mother and a father struck me. I don't mean to suggest that he was negligent in any way. But as a mother, I lived with a moment-to-moment awareness of my children. I knew what mood they were in from hour to hour, what they planned to do tomorrow, and next week, and next summer. There was not an instant or a corner of their lives that I wasn't intimately linked to. But there were so many moments of child rearing where he was absent. And this was not particular to Javad. He adored our daughters. In Iran, however, the mother is the pillar that holds up the family, always anticipating the needs and dangers around the bend. I do not think I have encountered in my life more than a handful of Iranian men who do not foist the responsibility of both the house and the children onto their wives. In addition to everything I had to do, I also had to teach my daughters the fine points of politics, how to conduct themselves in an unstable society.

*I*n Iran, overriding authority rests with the supreme religious leader, under the doctrine of divine clerical right to rule, *velayat-e faqih,* invented and established by Ayatollah Khomeini. It is his successor, Supreme Leader Ayatollah Ali Khamenei, who holds the real power in Iran. He heads the armed forces and appoints officials to influential state bodies, from the judiciary to the state media and, most important, the Guardian Council, a body that vets both new laws and elections. Under this system, branches of the government such as parliament and the executive function as accessories. If they are filled with officials whose politics complement the supreme leader's, they are allowed to pass laws and carry forth their agendas. If people elect a president or parliamentarians whose policies do not suit the (unelected) supreme leader, they are effectively discarded. Their reforms and laws are blocked in the labyrinth of the Islamic Republic's institutions.

On the sixth day of riots, President Khatami turned against the protesters. He accused them of "attacking the foundations of the regime and of wanting to foment tensions and disorders," and he warned them that they would be "repressed with force and determination."

Khatami's reaction stunned the student activists, who had believed that the moderate president would stand by them. Even among the students, many were certain that regime hard-liners had dispatched provocateurs into the crowds to chant incendiary slogans. Once the crowds had started chanting, "Death to the supreme leader," the security forces had cracked down and the protests had turned violent. Reformists, too, were convinced that the shift from protests to riots had been instigated. If student protests were seen as the natural precursors to mass street violence and a breakdown in social order, the reform movement would be reluctant to use one of its most important political tools: the ability to draw young people out into the streets.

Later President Khatami said that the whole debacle—from the attack on the dormitory itself to the dangerous and mysteriously escalating unrest—was the price he paid for holding the state accountable for the serial murders. After that summer, I felt that the president became permanently queasy, wary that pushing the boundaries would result in another hard-line provocation and crackdown. President Khatami, in the end, had been a librarian and a culture minister. That summer he witnessed students being killed on his watch, and forever after his focus shifted from changing Iran to preventing such a thing from happening again.

For me, and for all those who felt that the investigation into the serial killings could herald a new era of state accountability, that summer offered only profound disappointment. Powerful, shadowy hard-liners in the Islamic Republic seemed disinclined to fight their battles through the political process. They seemed as indifferent to the public opinion of Iranians and the world at large as ever. The immediate future suddenly looked bleaker. It was a time of reckoning for the reformists and the president, who confronted the steely fist of their hard-line opponents and realized how brutally real political challenge would be put down. What about their other dreams? Of tinkering with the constitution and amending its statutes to strengthen the hand of elected government? These were the sort of substantive and structural changes the reformists had in mind, what they felt was necessary to making Iran more democratic from the inside out. That summer was a turning point for the motley assortment of religious nationalists, secularists, former regime loyalists, and intellectuals loosely known as the reform movement. As has been the tendency of organized Iranian political groups from the beginning of time, the movement splintered, and then its splinters splintered. No one could agree anymore on tactics, let alone strategy. Call for a national referendum! Target the leadership in the press! Throw up your hands and advocate secularism! Move slowly! Hurry up!

CHAPTER TEN

A Conscientious Prisoner

IN THE COURSE OF HISTORY, CATACLYSMIC EVENTS ARE often remembered by one defining image. The photo of the lone Chinese student facing the tanks in Tiananmen Square. Boris Yeltsin on a Russian tank. In the case of the student riots of 1999, it was the picture of twenty-three-year-old Ahmad Batebi, a handsome young man with long dark brown locks and a black armband, holding aloft the bloody white shirt of a friend. Batebi was sentenced to death, and the friend whose shirt he was holding—well, that friend was already dead. He was one of the contested number killed, and his name was Ezzat Ebrahimnezhad.

One morning late in the summer of 1999, after the riots had been put down and life ground back to what passed for normal, I read in the newspaper that Ezzat's father was willing to sell his small house in the provinces to hire a lawyer to pursue his son's killers. It was so distressing to read of the old man's desperation that I tracked him down and offered my services for free. Several days later, Ezzat's sister arrived at my door wrapped in a black chador and slid into a chair with a great exhalation of relief. "I'm so glad," she said, "that you're a woman. It means I can travel from the village to see you without setting off the gossips." She was a war widow, she explained, and had already provoked a whisper campaign by enrolling in the university. She didn't need any more trouble.

A week later, she returned with her father, a grief-stricken old man carrying a book of Ezzat's poetry. "I didn't know," I said, "that Ezzat was a poet." "Oh yes," he told me, flipping through the pages with rough fingers. "Read this one." The poem was beautiful, and it contained a line where Ezzat concluded that he would die at the age of twenty-one. His family's description of Ezzat and his tragic death were too much for me. Talented, hardworking, and ambitious, Ezzat was the sort of young man Iran typically lost to the West, in a brain drain that grew each year. He had stayed and persevered, flourishing despite everything that young people in this country had working against them. To me, Ezzat embodied what made me proud of Iran's young people—how they chose resilience over anomie, their creativity in the face of dogma. And now he was dead, this graceful young poet with his somber verse and unsettling prescience. As a rule, I don't cry very much. But that day I excused myself, and sobbed in the bathroom until my eyes burned.

Several days later, the trial of the Tehran police chief and the officers present at the scene, who were charged with assault on the students, began at the military court. Dressed in civilian clothing, the police chief spent his whole time on the stand sweating profusely, bragging about his war record, and complaining that his spleen was acting up. At the end of the long, protracted trial, all the defendants were acquitted. Only one officer in the entire case was charged. And for what? Stealing an electric shaver from a dorm room. The verdict became a running joke among the students, a tragicomic climax rivaled only by the depilatory suicide of Saeed Emami, the death-squad chief: another wanton abrogation of justice in the name of hair removal.

✳ ✳ ✳

*I*n the weeks that followed, I pursued Ezzat's case, which was being tried separately. The more I learned details and pursued leads in the dark, the more disturbed I grew. One afternoon Ezzat's relatives came to my office, distraught after visiting his grave. While they were placing a wreath on his grave several days before, a group of hecklers had emerged from among the tombstones, cursing and hurling rocks at them. Frightened, they had hurried away. They had just gone back to recite prayers for him in peace. Again, as if out of nowhere, the grave stalkers had appeared, howling obscenities and pelting them with gravel and bits of dirt. Ezzat's sister reported that she had been barred from entering two government offices, and that a rumor was spreading in their village that they were anti-revolutionaries. "Even though," she sniffed, "I am war widow."

I became briefly optimistic after a student and a young female reporter tracked me down one day at my office. The student had been standing near Ezzat when he was shot, and had helped carry him to the hospital where he died a few hours later. The woman had also witnessed Ezzat being sprayed with bullets. Relieved to finally add heft to my case, I quickly included their accounts in the file. But after the two formally testified, the court abruptly changed course. The military court announced that it lacked jurisdiction over the matter and transferred it to the prosecutor's office, which similarly declared itself jurisdictionally unfit. The justice system passed the case back and forth until it was finally referred to the supreme court, to determine which branch had jurisdiction.

I realized that Ezzat's case would be consigned to an endless bureaucratic reordering unless I managed to find some evidence about those who had attacked the students. According to both the police and student witnesses, the mystery perpetrators throughout the protests were the *lebas-shakhsis*—literally, the plainclothesmen. The term is shorthand for the paramilitary forces in civilian clothes, the silent henchmen used by hard-line power centers in Iran to put down unrest, terrorize public spaces, and generally execute the more brutal schemes that ordinary police or security forces prefer to eschew. When they are sent on raids, they can be distinguished by their stubble, stocky build, and seedy watchfulness. It is unclear precisely who commands them or bankrolls their mercenary tactics. They are akin to a local Mafia that terrorizes a neighborhood, whispering threats in the ears of shop owners, staging violent hits that are designed to instill fear and a permanent sense of insecurity. Just as a film mafioso can be spotted from three blocks away, everyone could pick out the *lebas-shakhsis* immediately, but no one knew precisely who they were. How do you prosecute paramilitaries who melt into the dim alleys of the city after revving up their motorcycles and whirling maces above their heads? They operated with the tacit approval of the system, which declined to rein them in. But how to hold them accountable when technically they did not exist? It was like trying to prosecute a ghoul.

One morning in March 2000, a young man by the name of Amir Farshad Ebrahimi showed up at my office claiming to be a whistle-blower *lebas-shakhsi*. He said he had firsthand information about his comrades who had carried out the attack on the dormitory. He said he belonged to one of the most violent paramilitary groups, Ansar-e Hezbollah (of no relationship to the militant Lebanese group with a similar name), and that the group's chief had thrown him in prison for trying to resign from his unit. Was it not too good to be true? Details please, I said cautiously.

Once he started, Amir Farshad didn't stop. He himself, he said, had procured money and equipment for the attack, and had evidence about others involved. During the time he was active in the group, he had also been involved in violent attacks on two reformist ministers. If what he said was true, Amir Farshad was a jewel of a witness, not just for Ezzat's case but as a broader link to many shadowy attacks that had been left hanging for want of evidence. "Now that I want out," he said, "they're trying to frame me." It was like being in a gang, he explained; you could not simply exit. Your knowledge made you a liability. They imprisoned him for seven months, he told me, and tortured him. Once, they stuck him in a narrow closet the size of a coffin and left him there for twenty-four hours.

"Amir Farshad," I said, "you need to go public with what you know. It's safer for you that way. Your secrets are dangerous to you as secrets, but once they are out in the public realm, it's over." He agreed, and we made arrangements to videotape his testimony. I made sure to plan all the details in person, since I knew my phones were tapped. And I asked two people to join us as witnesses, in case it was alleged later that I had somehow enticed or forced Amir Farshad's disclosures. On the day of our appointment, I opened the door to Amir Farshad and his sister, and stared at her in bewilderment. Maybe Amir Farshad was a whistle-blower, but he had still been devout enough to join a paramilitary group Taliban-like in its radical interpretation of Islam. It would only make sense for his sister to wear the black chador, or at least dress conservatively. Instead she wore makeup and daintily offered me a hand with manicured fuchsia nails. Odd, I thought.

We moved to the room where the witnesses were waiting, and after taking down a plaque and other telltale signs that would identify the locale as my office, I began filming his testimony. When we finished, one of the witnesses, a researcher from an American human rights group, called me into the other room. "Shirin," she said urgently, "this is a trap. If Amir Farshad really wants to testify, why hasn't he gone to the government? The government is currently controlled by reformists, after all, who would be sympathetic. Why has he come to you? You could be arrested for this video. They could charge you with falsifying information against the Islamic Republic."

"I'm not doing anything illegal," I replied. "I'm a lawyer, gathering evidence for my case."

But her warning made me think. And, frankly, I was disquieted. I decided I didn't want that tape on my hands. The next day, I drove over to the office of the deputy interior minister and left it with him.

I figured that even if it was a trap, at least the videotape was no longer in my possession.

Several days later, articles began surfacing in the newspapers about a videotape circulating in Tehran and abroad in which a young man exposed the activities of the notorious Ansar-e Hezbollah. The articles worried me, especially when they began appearing in the hard-line press, which hinted that two lawyers were responsible and ran an interview with Amir Farshad's mother in which she claimed that her son was emotionally unstable and had been brainwashed into making the revelations. Meanwhile, Amir Farshad himself had disappeared. His father said that their house had been raided and that agents had taken him away. "I've fallen into the very hands of those I was running from," Amir Farshad had whispered to his father as they'd hauled him into a waiting car.

The ensuing days were tension-filled and worrisome. The situation was spiraling out of control. Each day the hard-line papers ran attacks on those who were blemishing the revolution with this concocted tape. A court case was convened, and I was summoned for interrogation. Each day, I grew more anxious, convinced that it had all been a trap, certain that it would end with me going to prison.

The night after my second interrogation, some friends and relatives came over to celebrate my birthday. I smiled tightly the whole evening, passing out chocolate cake and pretending that nothing was wrong. But my mind kept straying to thoughts of prison and, most of all, of how my family would cope. That night, after putting on my pajamas and getting ready for bed, I sat at my desk and composed a letter to my family:

My dear ones,

By the time you read this, I will already be in prison. I want to assure you that I will fine. I will be released and unharmed, because I have done nothing wrong. Can you please do something for me? I want

*you to imagine for a moment that I've suffered a heart attack and have
been rushed to the hospital. Wouldn't that be terrible? It would be much,
much worse than my arrest. So please keep all this in perspective.*

Ghorban-e hamegi, *with love to all,*
Shirin

I handed the letter to Javad, who knew very little about all the events
that had transpired. He scanned it quickly, then looked up at me
quizzically. "Um, Shirin *jan*," he asked, "can you please explain what's
going on?" I tried to tell the story without sounding gloomy. "And," I
said, "you can read this aloud to the family as a consolation."

I tend to begin a lot of my sentences with the Persian equivalent of
"for better or for worse," which is something like "fortunately or unfortunately." It is not that I'm given to wobbling preambles, but so
much of what you experience under the Islamic Republic leaves you
at a loss, unable to apply objective measures. It is as though you are
constantly viewing reality through shattered fun-house mirrors, and
what looks tall or wide becomes so relative that you start to abandon
objective categories altogether: tall or wide? fortunate or unfortunate? Who knows.

So fortunately or unfortunately, when you are about to be arrested in the Islamic Republic, you get advance warning in the hard-
line press. Just as you might turn to a certain page for the week's
weather forecast or pick up the popular daily *Hamshahri* for classified
ads, you can scan the front pages of two or three hard-line papers as
a guide to whose arrest is on the way. If the headlines fall below the
fold or appear intermittently, the handcuffs are a good two or three
weeks away. If the libel against you is making the front page every
day, if the fury has become palpable in the top headlines, you know
you should pack your overnight bag.

Fortunately or unfortunately, the hard-line apparatus is media savvy; it sends out the equivalent of press releases early, to ensure that Western media outlets with deadlines across time zones can catch the news. It forgets to embargo their release until the actual hour of the arrest, which is how phone calls such as one I received on an early morning in June come to pass.

"Hello?" I said.

"Hello?" repeated the caller. "Who is this?"

"This is Shirin Ebadi."

"Mrs. Ebadi! I'm so happy to hear your voice! We received a telex earlier saying you had been arrested—"

"Really? You don't say . . ."

That day the phone did not stop ringing. For hours I repeated over and over to journalists that indeed I was not in prison. Yet. Even my sister called, after hearing a news bulletin on a Persian-language European radio station. "It's all a mistake," I assured her.

At five o'clock that afternoon, June 28, 2000, the phone call I had been waiting for finally came. "Please report to Branch 16 of the Tehran General Court," the caller said. This meant the time had come. I would be going to Evin.

As I made a last-minute survey of the apartment, checking to be sure I had packed my blood-pressure medication and an extra toothbrush, I convinced myself I would be back soon. "Your father and I have a meeting this evening," I called out to the girls, who were watching television in the living room. "Order yourselves a pizza for dinner." I was anxious that Javad not linger too long at the ministry, where I had been ordered to report first, in case our daughters started to worry.

The session with the court judge lasted no longer than twenty minutes. He promised to alert my husband, who I presumed was waiting outside, that I had been taken to prison. The guards led me to a parking lot I had never seen before, through a back door. It was quite late, after ten, and the fluorescent streetlights bathed the parking lot in a strange orange glow. The traffic had slowed by that hour, so it didn't take long to drive up the expressway, past the spiraling twin minarets of the new praying grounds and the elaborate YA HOSSEIN written out in electric lights on a nearby hillside. The driver stopped at a kiosk along the way and bought me a soda. My mouth had gone dry.

Finally we reached Evin. Evin, through whose barbed-wire gates almost every political prisoner in the last half century has passed. Evin, where my brother-in-law Fuad spent the last years of his youth. My thoughts swirled back to earlier times, to the looming presence of Evin in our history. I was wholly unprepared for the first question I was asked upon my arrival:

"Are you here for a moral offense?"

Women who are arrested and brought to Evin after dark are typically prostitutes. After a second of shock, I realized that the prison guard assumed that this might be the case with me.

"No! What are you talking about? My offense is political!"

I was reminded of a joke we always told whose punch line was "My crime is political." I started to laugh, which incensed the prison official to no end. "Why are you laughing?" he demanded, irate.

"My crime is political," I kept repeating, my laughter bordering on hysteria. He waited for me to compose myself, then just looked away in disgust when he saw that I could not.

"Just write down anything, and take her away."

A female guard guided me down a long corridor, to what she referred to as her "best cell." A friend of mine, another female lawyer, had been detained a few weeks earlier, and jokingly she'd told me that she had asked them to reserve her own cell, their "best," for me. And now here I was. The best cell was covered in filth, and the sink had no running water. Dirt and rust rimmed the metal toilet in the corner. "Is there a better one?" I asked tentatively. She let me peer into three others, and I realized grimly that mine was indeed less bad. Unable to work up the courage to go back into it yet, I sat hunched in the corridor. A few female prisoners in the same ward passed by on the way to washing their dishes. "What are you in for?" they asked. The case of Amir Farshad had been dubbed "the case of the tapemakers" in the press, so without raising my head, I just whispered, "The tapemakers."

"Really? What was it called?" one asked. "How much did you get paid?" "Was the director nice?" the others wanted to know.

Oh my goodness, I thought to myself, they think I'm here for making a porn movie. I lowered my head again and tried to drown out their crass voices.

A bit later, the prison doctor stopped by my cell to measure my blood pressure. When he left, clanging the door behind him, I gazed at the pocked, stained walls of the cell and felt all of the anxiety of the previous weeks slowly ebbing away. I had no recourse to anyone or anything, I realized, except God. "I've done everything I could do," I whispered, "and now it's Your turn." Then I made a pillow out of my bag, pulled my chador over me, and fell asleep.

The clank of the metal breakfast tray woke me up. A piece of bread, a small square of salty cheese, and some tea. A guard rapped on my door and summoned me to be properly checked in. She tossed me a prison chador—blue, with a mocking pattern of the scales of justice—and instructed me to follow her. Down in the administrative office, they fingerprinted me, hung a numbered tag around my head, and took mug shots. One of the guards asked me, "So what do you play?" In Iran, when someone is arrested, their house is also raided for evidence. Since some of the ayatollahs consider playing musical instruments immoral, I thought they had found the girls' piano or my husband's sitar and were trying to add playing music to the list of my offenses. "I don't play anything at all," I sniffed.

"Stop fooling around," the guard snapped. "We're already tired of your games from last night. Now I'm asking you again: What do you play?"

"The piano belongs to my daughters," I said. "Not everyone is musically inclined, you know."

The guard who had escorted me down here caught the misunderstanding and, with a faint smile, explained to the first guard that I had been arrested in relation to the Amir Farshad case.

Again, the truth dawned on me. He had thought I was a drug addict! In Persian, the verb used for doing drugs is the same as that used for playing a musical instrument. "What do you play?" also means "What do you take?"—as in drugs. He had assumed I was high last night, to have laughed so hysterically. Prostitute, porn star, drug addict. Did no one in this prison think a woman could be a prisoner of conscience?!

After the booking, I was taken to a new cell. It was no upgrade, but at least the guards were kinder, and I noticed that they were treating me specially. They scooped out bowls of food from a huge pot for the other inmates but served me a special tray of *chelo-kabob*. For a few hours I stared at the ceiling, then at the floor, and then felt myself going cross-eyed from boredom. So I started peeping through the little hole in the door. One of the prisoners had her child with her, and she was playing in the halls, entertaining the guards.

The guards, it turned out, all had college degrees, with backgrounds in juvenile reform. They knew of a children's rights organization I had helped found, and when they discovered the connection, they turned even more respectful and sweet. They snuck me into the prison library so I could get some books. (It was technically reserved for male inmates; even here, we were second-class.) They brought me fresh clothes. But they couldn't protect me from the luridness of the night. Many of the prisoners in my solitary ward were drug addicts and had been brought there to quit their addiction without the aid of any detoxification drugs. They howled and screeched through the night, horrible screams that reverberated through the walls, worse than injured wolves or anything else I could imagine. The guards began feeling cozy with me, and would sometimes come and sit in my cell to complain about their jobs. I sympathized. It was tough work. But at least you get to go home after your shift, I thought to myself.

It was so odd to me, how the rhythm of prison life became familiar. The personality quirks of the guards, the dank, dusty smell of the cells, even the howls of the addicts seemed normal to me after a couple of days. On the third day, a young man visited my cell and accused me of trying to pass a phone number out of prison. "I've done no such thing," I said politely. He grew furious and searched my bag, with rough, jerky movements. I was dumbfounded. The prison guard, an affectionate woman whom I had gotten to know a little, came to my cell afterward.

"Why the hell didn't you defend yourself?" she demanded, her eyes full of reproach. "Why didn't you tell him the guards here have reported no such thing? What the hell was he talking about? What kind of damn law school did you go to? What's the point of all that law education if you just sit there silently."

I said nothing, just closed my eyes as though tired. I was too worn out to argue with her. Too dejected to explain that a legal defense is of use only in places where due process is respected. She touched my shoulder, sighed softly, telling me to trust in God, and let me be.

Later that night, a sharp rap on the door jolted me alert from my half-conscious stupor. "Get ready, you're being sent to another prison," a woman's voice announced from the other side of the door. Suddenly, all the fear that I had managed to fight back since arriving at Evin rushed me at once. As I picked up my bag with trembling fingers, snatches of all the reports on prison torture I had read began flashing through my mind.

Calm down, I instructed myself rather uselessly. I knew they wouldn't dare rape me. But I knew they could lash my bare feet with electric cables until I "confessed," until I said, "Yes, I, Shirin Ebadi, falsified propaganda against the Islamic Republic."

"Where are you taking me?" I asked. Silence. "Please, can you please just tell me where we're going?" What if they were taking me to the dreaded place known by the ominous bland title of the Joint Committee? Torture there was rampant. If that's where we were going, then I would know what lay in store.

No one would answer me. "Just walk," they said. At a dark court-yard in front of the prison block, a bus stood waiting. One of the guards tied a blindfold around my head and helped me onto the bus. We rumbled off, and I groped the seat beneath me, staring into the blackness of the folded cloth over my eyes. We seemed to be driving around in circles. When we stopped, I stumbled out of the bus, my hands floating in front of me. "This way," someone said. I recognized the voice. It was Ali, my interrogator at the court. "We're convening a court session for you," he said. My hand was placed on the stump of what felt like a staff. "Follow me."

I tried to, blind, guided only by a staff, with vivid images of all the hideous things that could go wrong flitting through my mind. My mouth went dry, and I couldn't stay quiet. "You will have to answer on Judgment Day," I cried shrilly to Ali. "It is you who are the negligent one! You are supposedly my interrogator, meant to investigate this. But instead of tracing who actually leaked the tape, you're simply charging me." I was beside myself, fury and terror dissolving all my inhibitions. My voice pitched high, I practically screamed, "I want you to know, I will *never, ever* forgive you on Judgment Day."

Suddenly, the staff halted. "Take off the blindfold," Ali said. I blinked, my eyes adjusting to the dim light of a narrow hallway, about the width of a large man's shoulders. Eight doors opened off the corridor, to eight solitary cells. "The water here is cleaner," he said (the contaminated well water in the other ward had upset my stomach), "the food is better, and no one will disturb you at night. You'll be much more comfortable," he promised. "I think I would be more comfortable at home," I answered sullenly. "Why am I here in the first place?" He turned on his heels without answering me, strode out of the hallway, and locked the door behind him.

I began investigating my new surroundings. There was no guard. I peered into each cell, each of them windowless, carpeted with grimy, cheap fabric that had clearly been used and unwashed for years. In one of the rooms, my eyes seized upon a half-full pack of cheap Iranian cigarettes. I really, really wanted to smoke. I left a crumpled bill on the table, as we were allowed to keep some money on us to use at the prison sundries kiosk, and went foraging for matches. For half an hour, I inspected each cell, checking in corners, under the carpet, everywhere. Smoking is permitted in prison, but inmates aren't allowed to keep their own matches or lighters. You have to rap on your cell door and ask one of the guards to come light your cigarette for you. I wanted to smoke one of those cigarettes as badly as I had ever wanted anything. But I had promised myself I would never request anything in prison. It was a point of principle. I refused to need anything it was in their power to give. After another fruitless search, I threw the pack back on the table, curled up on the stinking floor, and went to sleep.

The kick to my side was delivered to hurt, as well as to wake me up. "What are you doing here?" A stout woman with oily skin towered above me.

"I don't know," I said sleepily. "They brought me here last night."

"Well, this is the guard's room, so you can take yourself else-where."

"Fine," I said, gathering my things.

"What are you in for anyway?" she asked with an offhand rude-ness.

None of your business, I wanted to retort. But I lectured myself: You're stuck here, you'll need to somehow win these awful people over. I explained calmly.

"You're lying," she said, rummaging through my bag. She took away my clothes and tossed a smelly, stained chador in my direction.

"But . . . but . . . please give me my own clothes back."

"That's all you're going to get," she snapped.

Later a doctor came to check my blood pressure, and I petitioned him for my own clothes. For some reason, it made a universe of difference, sitting in that cell in my own clean dress instead of in the foul, unwashed smock worn by a hundred wretched women.

I couldn't decide whether I preferred the old ward or the new. Here, the menu was improved. Chicken kabobs, schnitzel, nutritious stews, and, every ten days, an apple! But the guards were enthusiastically ill-tempered, mean, and petty; there were four of them guarding just me, and they resented this fact greatly. "*We* are *your* prisoners," they liked to say. It was difficult to tell what time of day it was, since the naked lightbulb hanging in my cell was always on and there were no windows by which to detect dawn or dusk. I was allowed no newspapers, no radio. Sometimes I would wake from a nap and wonder whether ten minutes or ten hours had passed. It was disorienting, which I suppose was the point.

After the first day in the new ward, I began to go mad from the loneliness and the silence. I missed my ex-neighbors cursing and swearing, their middle-of-the-night howls for "just a bit of heroin" and their banging against the iron door for a light for a cigarette. After a day, my claustrophobia and agitation passed. Hmmm, I thought to myself, maybe Evin isn't all that bad. At least I didn't have to think about mopping the floors or taking out the garbage. I didn't need to worry about the article I had promised to write or the trial I should be preparing for. There were no students asking me if I'd had a chance to look at their theses. No dinner to cook. No mortgage to pay.

My interrogations usually took place in a small room nearly filled by a dilapidated wooden table. The sessions lasted several hours, the circuitous questions repeated themselves, and the judge began each round with a sonorous recitation of Koranic verse. My interrogator, Ali, was also on hand, and all in all, they were both courteous enough. What flustered me was not so much the interrogations but the slowing of time. Hours turned to days, and days turned to weeks in the suffocating sameness of my cell. I prayed five times a day. I stretched and attempted calisthenics.

One morning, out of nowhere, the guard handing me breakfast said I should dress for my trial that day. The prospect of leaving the confines of the cell block for anywhere at all, even what would be a flawed trial, shot my heart through with joy. I boarded a little minibus only to find Amir Farshad himself, as well as two others involved in the case, on board, dressed in prison uniforms and slippers. The moment we entered the courthouse, I was overwhelmed by an intense feeling of overstimulation. After being alone, or with a guard or an interrogator, for the last several hundred hours, the throngs of people—well-wishers, journalists pushing against police officers to speak to us—flooded my senses with shouts and colors.

Suddenly I heard my husband's familiar voice trying to attract my attention. He pushed his way forward, along with the lawyer who would be representing me. It turned out to be just a preliminary session. Amir Farshad was put on the stand, and he courageously stayed loyal to his original story. Then the court read the complaints of the plaintiffs, who were basically a selection of the extremist right, paramilitaries, and the hard-line press. At one point during Amir Farshad's testimony, the judge summoned Ali, the interrogator.

"His testimony doesn't match the transcript of his interrogation," the judge said.

"Let me try to remind him," Ali replied.

This conversation was had within earshot. As we were herded out of the courtroom, I caught sight of my teary-eyed sister pushing toward the front. She couldn't manage to get through the crush of people, but our eyes locked.

Ten more days in prison. Ten more days of clanking breakfast trays, of sullen guards smoking and despising me for a oneness that required the supervision of their four. Ten more days of trying to imagine the gentle, rocky slope of the Alborz Mountains behind Evin, where my poet friend Simin Behbahani and I hiked each week, talking languorously while we scaled the mountain, as teenagers scampered past us with their boom boxes and jaunty bandannas. We usually climbed to a particular summit and stopped for tea at its mountainside café, savoring the cool alpine air and the vista of a lush green gorge. Simin and I are kindred spirits, and many of the themes of her poetry—women's suffering, the celebration of their rights and existence—inspire my own work. I tried to force more hours to pass by remembering lines of her *ghazals.* The images came, of monsters soaring the sky in trails of smoke, of plundered mermaids.

In those last days, I started to hallucinate. All my niggling physical ailments suddenly acted up. My hip pains, hypertension, heart palpitations—even my childhood stutter returned. I despised my own weakness and tried not to complain. I just pressed my teeth together, flexed my fingers until the nails turned blue, and bit back my groans. I tried to remember who had said, "We are not born to suffer." I couldn't, however, and my inability to recall made me terribly angry. I picked up a metal spoon and began trying to carve some words into the cell's cement wall: "We are born to suffer because we are born in the Third World. Space and time are imposed on us. There is nothing to do but stay patient."

I tried not to get too dreamy, so that I would be crystal-sharp and alert during the interrogations. It was not uncommon for the interrogating judge to bluff and corner you into implicating someone, by suggesting that the person had implicated you first. An unsubtle and classic ploy of interrogation; I managed to evade each attempt. Others involved in the case did not. One of them in the end implicated me. I tried to convince myself not to judge him for this. After all, people cope with interrogation and torture differently. People have different constitutions, temperaments, and sensibilities; some have spent their whole lives anticipating the day they'll be strapped to a table, getting their feet lashed by a cruel cord, being instructed, in between lashes, to name names, to blurt it all out. But even hard-core political activists who've braced themselves for either physical or psychological intimidation won't know until it comes to pass whether, or for how long, they can hold out.

Sometimes I think this is one of the saddest realities of being an activist or an intellectual in a place like Iran. When dissidents or just regular old intellectuals come out of prison, often they are not celebrated for simply being brave and having survived but are pruriently examined for their conduct in prison. Did they succumb and agree to videotaped confessions? Did they sign letters? Did they make lists of their comrades? By judging what ethically should be immune from judgment—the response of an individual to a form of torture—we enable the interrogator's tactics. We legitimize the sickness of the whole enterprise, as though when forced into the wretched position of sustaining torture or breaking down, there is such thing as a right response.

The second session of the trial unfolded much like the first. At least this time the court permitted my husband to speak to me for a few minutes in the hallway. "Do not, under any circumstances," I said, "let my mother or the girls visit me in prison." I woke up every morning thinking about them, but I didn't want them to see me in a prison uniform, behind bars. I didn't want them to have to live with that memory. My sister rushed up as the guard was taking me away and followed us, whispering, "Are you okay? Are you okay?" in my ear. The next day, Javad was allowed to come see me in prison. We spoke very briefly, and before leaving he slipped a novel I had left unfinished on the bedside, *The Fig Tree of the Monasteries,* into my hand.

On an indolent Thursday evening, as I lay restless on the soiled carpet of my cell, too sleepy to read but too anxious to sleep, the guard rapped at my door and announced that I had a phone call. It was the judge presiding over my case, calling to say that twenty-five days after I had first passed through the iron gates of Evin Prison, I could be released on twenty million *toman* bail (about $25,000). Euphoric, I immediately dialed my home number and asked my husband to show up at the courthouse first thing Saturday morning, with the deed to our house.

The next day, the hours crept by with agonizing slowness, but the news of my release had calmed me, and I found myself able to concentrate on the novel for the first time. When night fell, and the book felt heavy in my hand, I lay on my back and let my mind wander. I thought of seeing my daughters again, and of how relieved I was that they had been spared the sight of me in a dirty prison chador. I thought of the weekly hikes I would resume with my poet friend, setting out at first light and stopping for tea beside a snow-dusted ravine, Tehran receding in the distance. I thought of what one of my clients, Akbar Ganji, once told me about the indispensability of prison. In Iran, he'd warned, unless you are punished before the public, everyone will assume that you collaborate with the regime.

When I woke up Saturday morning, I took a long look around the cell whose contours I had memorized, and wondered how long it would take to forget the shapes of the stains, the graffiti carved on the walls. By nine A.M., having packed the five or so items that constituted my personal belongings, I sat ready on the cot, waiting eagerly for the guard's knock. At five o'clock, it finally came. The burly guard, the one who had complained of being my prisoner, swung the cell door open and told me to follow her. She moved laboriously down the corridor, and I willed myself to stay at her pace, though my feet felt so light I thought they might take off underneath me at any moment.

In the courtyard of the prison, an ambulance with tinted windows idled in wait. A prison official told me that it would drop me off at a taxi service. Why an ambulance? Tehran traffic is unmoved by emergency vehicles, so surely not for the sake of transporting me more quickly. I thought it better not to ask questions at that point and simply got into the ambulance. As we rolled out onto the crowded expressway, I gazed affectionately at the snarl of cars—bored drivers checking out those around them, dusty trucks loaded with fruit, playful comments painted on their sides—and thought, for the first time ever, that six o'clock traffic in Tehran was not without its charms.

Before long, we reached the yawning juncture in north Tehran, crisscrossed above by overpasses, known as the Parkway intersection. While stopped at the red light, the "ambulance driver" called down to the taxi beside us and asked if the cabbie could take me home. Surprised, the driver nodded, and I grabbed my bag and jumped out.

"Are you ill, *khanum*?" he asked, staring at me in his rearview mirror.

"No," I said, "I've just been released from prison!" He looked startled, so I quickly told him not to worry. "I'm not a thief or a criminal," I said. "I was a political prisoner."

He studied my face closely, then exclaimed, "Hey! Aren't you *Khanum* Ebadi?" When I said yes, he smiled brightly and congratulated me on being freed. After a polite two-minute wait, he launched into his own tale of woe. He had a master's degree in engineering and supplemented his tiny income by renting a friend's cab in the afternoon. He lamented corruption and bribery, inflation and joblessness. After a while, he stopped checking to see if I was listening. He seemed even sadder than I was.

I was eager to get home, but I could not resist stopping at one of the white clapboard kiosks along the way for newspapers, the daily ritual I had missed the most in prison. I surveyed the stacks—laid out on the sidewalk like a quilt, there were so many—with greedy eyes. I bought seven or eight, rolled them together, and pressed them tightly against my chest. As the taxi began the slow descent down my sloped street, I could see my relatives gathered outside the house, with a lamb ready for sacrifice. The driver rushed around to open my door, and refused to take any money from me.

As I walked through the door, my daughters hurled themselves into my arms, squeezing me tight for a long minute. That night we stayed up late, drinking round after round of tea. My husband placed before me a great stack of newspapers, all those printed during my time in prison, and I began rifling through them as the conversation buzzed around me. My daughters sat beside me, breathless from filling me in on all that had transpired in their lives while I had been gone. They were used to consulting with me on everything, from homework to friends to which way they should part their hair, and now they recounted all the decisions, minor and major, they had made on their own in my absence.

They had also amassed messages from everyone who had called or faxed from around the world since the news of my imprisonment, and the bulk of the folder surprised even me. My international reputation had grown slowly over many years, and it was not every day I had such a thick stack of messages to remind me just how far and wide it had been established.

After I had looked over the last of the notes, well past midnight, the relatives began leaving one by one, and a warm quiet descended on the living room where we sat. I had made it a practice for years to keep the uglier side of my work out of the house. I never spoke much about my cases, for many of them involved defending victims of horrific violence, and I saw no reason why my daughters should be exposed to all the painful details. Of course they overheard me giving interviews on the phone, and they knew my workdays were filled with trials and trips to prison to visit clients. But I felt it was important to maintain some balance and draw some boundaries around my work. To the extent I could manage, I kept our dinner conversations light, teased my daughters, and tried to encourage something resembling a normal atmosphere. Coming out of prison was just a more challenging moment in a long-running effort to pretend that at home I was a mom like all others. Starting the next morning, I acted as though I had simply been away for a conference, and save the fact that I had brought back no gifts from this trip, within a day we all went about the house as though this had truly been the case.

I am sure you have a hundred questions. What did it all mean? What happened to Ezzat? What happened to my case? Ezzat's case, for which I went to prison, was ultimately dismissed. The revolutionary court announced that since no people had officially been charged and since Ezzat was dead anyway, the case was closed. So the judges shut their books, but in the minds of Iranians the case remained wide open, as it remains to this day.

What is the legacy of it all? What was the lasting impact of the worst unrest since the 1979 revolution, of the case of Ezzat Ebrahimnezhad, a young poet who was shot by paramilitaries the state permits to prey upon its citizens? I am often asked, Why do Iranian young people simply not rise up? If their discontent is so deep, their alienation so irreversible, if they are 70 percent of Iranian society, what explains their complacency?

But just look. Look at how high the personal price of protest. Ezzat protested against a newspaper's closure and was killed in a dormitory. Imagine what is reserved for students bold enough to organize and hold sit-ins, students who are overtly political. The main student organization in Iran in recent years routinely complains that in those dark days of 1999, everyone—from the so-called reformists to President Khatami himself—abandoned them. That Ezzat, the victim, was branded an agitator, that in the trials that followed not a single attacker was brought to justice.

Was there another legacy? Could we draw a line after 1999 and say that after this year the Islamic Republic definitively changed in some way? You could say that the regime, for so long out of touch, was forced to confront the depths of people's discontent.

What about young Ahmad Batebi, the student in the picture holding up Ezzat's bloodstained shirt, with whom we began this story? The young man with the coffee-bean eyes and red bandanna, whose Che Guevara looks made the photo even more memorable. The supreme leader stayed his execution and reduced his sentence to fifteen years. He came to visit me one day, on one of his furloughs from prison. He had put on weight, and his hair was shorter than in that famous picture. His very body language radiated defeat.

"They wrote 'Ahmad Batebi' on my arm in marker, had me fill out a will, and blindfolded me. They took me into a room and forced me to kneel. A shot rang out. I fainted. When I came to, I found myself lying on the floor, and I wondered, 'Is this the afterlife? If so, why does the afterlife look like my prison cell?' I started slamming my elbows against the cement walls, thinking, If I'm dead, then of course I won't feel pain. I was innocent when I went into that prison. Innocent not just of a crime but as a human being. Maybe I'll be free one day. But my future was lost inside the walls of that prison. After what I saw, after what they did to me, how can I ever be a person again?"

He was the same age as my older daughter. As he sat on my couch, telling his broken story, all I could think was, What if this had happened to my daughter? What in God's name would I have done?

CHAPTER ELEVEN

In the Shadows of Reform

DO YOU WANT A CHOCOLATE CAKE OR COFFEE MOUSSE? I asked my daughter Negar, who was turning twenty-three at the end of the week. We sat at the small table in the kitchen, making a list of what we needed to buy before her party. I would make salad *olivieh,* a hearty potato salad; *kotlet,* small patties of ground meat and potatoes; and some dips that her friends could graze on throughout the evening. At the very end of the night, once they were tired of talking and dancing and turning up the music, I would serve the cake, with little bowls of Persian ice cream, the saffron kind flecked with pistachios and perfumed with rose water. "Am I forgetting anyone?" Negar asked, running up and down the list, twirling a lock of her long brown hair around a finger. "They should come around nine, right?"

Planning a birthday party in 2003 was an altogether different enterprise than in the nineties, when they were, like any gathering of young people, a cause for great anxiety. Back then, I would encourage the girls to invite their friends over early, so they could turn the music up in the early evening, when the streets were still loud with traffic. I tried to serve dinner after ten, so the kids would be busy eating then and less inclined to blast the stereo when it could be heard easily from the top of the street. Usually this met with limited success, because inevitably the volume knob would turn itself up until the house pulsed, and I was sure the whole neighborhood could hear. I would make my husband go outside and walk a hundred yards up the block, to see how far the noise reached. By the time we lit candles and cut the cake, I was more worried than I would let on, and half the birthday pictures we have in our album feature me with a tense smile on my lips.

Those years were behind us now. Happily, my daughters' late adolescence coincided with Iran's reform years, the eight-year stretch beginning in 1997, when the moderate President Khatami sought to pull back the system's interference in people's private lives. I was grateful for this, for I could not imagine parenting teenagers in the repressive years that preceded his tenure. In the early and mid-nineties, young people faced a social landscape bleak in its isolation from global culture and its dearth of opportunities for even modest forms of entertainment. The Internet had not yet penetrated Iranian homes and universities, restrictions on women's dress were rigidly enforced, and public space remained very much a charged and potentially hostile realm. Young people risked being intercepted by the morality police simply for venturing into the mountains together for a hike. Wearing anything but dark tones like navy and black opened young women up to harassment from the police, and a smudge of makeup or even light nail polish could be grounds for detainment or lashing.

The reform era, for all its political discontents, did much to relax our daily lives. The morality police were by no means retired, but they went from omnipresent invaders to a periodic nuisance. President Khatami deserves only a measure of credit for this shift. Really it was because my daughters' uncowed generation started fighting back and, through the force of their sheer numbers and boldness, made it unfeasible for the state to impose itself as before. Now plan-

ning a birthday party no longer required a battle strategy of timing
and defensive maneuvers. I no longer had to worry if the girls left the
house in sandals without socks, or wearing veils in bright hues. If
they were riding with a male cousin to a family dinner, I no longer
began to panic if they were ten minutes late, fearing a catastrophic
encounter at a checkpoint.

It was still inconceivable to socialize with real enjoyment in public. Sometimes I would hear my daughters playing albums of old Iranian singers, the ones who had transplanted themselves to Los Angeles
over two decades ago. "That's Mahasti, isn't it?" I would ask. "Or
maybe Haideh?" They would look at me with disbelief. "Maman,
how could *you* know that?" As though those disembodied voices coming out of the stereo had not once been live performers who sang in
the restaurants and hotels of Tehran. It was difficult for my daughters,
and for most young people, to fathom such a time, because this
Iran—the one where a woman's singing voice was forbidden in public—was the only reality they had ever known. For them, being able to
attend unmolested birthday parties and not being stopped at a checkpoint on the road to the ski slopes was progress.

The gradual dwindling of harassment revived public culture in
Tehran, and cafés sprouted up around the city, parks featured out-
door concerts, and new galleries opened up and mounted regular ex-
hibits. The Internet connected young people through chat rooms
and Weblogs, and for a while it seemed that much of young Tehran
was linked through friend network sites such as orkut.com. Although
a thick layer of smog still hung over the city, although paramilitaries
on motorbikes still intimidated young people on Friday mornings as
they headed to the mountains, although we still heard of the occasional party or coffee-shop raid, the city as experienced by a young
woman of twenty-two was still a more vibrant and tolerant place
than the Tehran of the early nineties.

These transformations, however, in no way checked Iran's brain
drain. Universities still turned out hundreds of thousands of skilled

graduates into a job market paltry with opportunity, and little chance of real advancement. Ambitious young people still believed the West offered them a more fulfilling and remunerative future, and left in droves. That year, my own Negar faced the choice of moving to Canada for graduate school.

We spent weeks debating the decision, lingering around the dinner table and letting the answering machine pick up the phone as we confronted the possibility that our family—close-knit, even by Iranian standards—might be separated by continents, perhaps forever. If Negar stayed in Iran, she could find a job and, like most Iranian young people, would discover that her salary would not cover even half the rent of a modest apartment. She could go on to study for her doctorate here, but the training she would receive would scarcely compare with that in the West's institutions of higher learning. Also, as with so many opportunities in Iran, entrance to doctoral programs was based on political connections, and I worried that because she was my daughter, state universities might reject her application.

If it were simply a matter of which country would make the finest electrical engineering PhD out of my daughter, the choice would be easy. But there was so much more to worry about than that. Of course I wanted Negar to reach her full potential professionally, but I also knew that after she'd experienced the freedom and comfort of life in the West, it might not be immediately clear to her that she could live in Iran again. For a bright young woman in her late twenties, the age she would be upon finishing graduate school, the chance to finally put her years of education to work in a competitive environment in one of the world's most beautiful cities would be difficult to turn down. I knew it wouldn't be Montreal's sidewalks cafés and summer jazz festivals that might keep her there. It would be the chance to work in an atmosphere where her contribution was respected, where she was constantly learning from her colleagues. How seductive it would be, I thought, for her to wake up in the morning, put on a crisp suit, and walk down a bustling street without a veil, feeling herself part of a global culture that was dynamic and full of life. How could she not want that for herself? How could I not want that for her, this daughter who had spent the last decade bent over her homework, who clearly excelled at and loved learning?

I struggled to put my selfishness aside when I suggested to Negar that there would also be drawbacks. I didn't want to discourage her, as it is hard enough for a young woman to make such a life choice, but I wanted her to know that staying abroad would complicate her emotional and personal life as surely as it would enhance her scholarship. Initial loneliness and pangs of estrangement aside, Negar would find herself in a city with a slim population of Iranians. Her twenties, the years in which she would meet lots of like-minded friends and colleagues and ideally choose a partner among them, would be spent among a small circle of limited prospects. In Tehran, at least, there would be many circles to choose from.

In the end, we decided that she should go. Once the decision was made, I pushed down my doubts and kept reminding all of us that it was not a terminal separation. The night she left, a temperate evening at the end of the summer, I pulled out the Koran and held it high in the door frame, so that she could pass beneath it three times on her way out, a ritual of departure we have performed too many times for our loved ones since the revolution. Her father and I drove her to the airport, taking the expressway south, past the towering murals of bearded, somber war martyrs, the billboards championing the Palestinian intifadah. We turned down the tree-lined four-lane road leading to the airport, continued past the terminal reserved for the hajj, or the pilgrimage to Mecca, and parked at the familiar gray main edifice of Mehrabad Airport, the scene of so many painful departures over these long years. Soon the government would open its new Imam Khomeini International Airport on the outskirts of Saveh, a town south of Tehran, but for now we still traveled from Mehrabad, faded but steeped in history, pressed cozily against the southern edge of the city. Families overran the small parking lot, searching for rusted, ramshackle baggage trolleys, laden with either bags or bouquets of flowers. Mullahs in full robes and turbans strode by, as did men in elegant business suits, women swathed in black chadors, women in pointy heels and sheer veils.

As I walked Negar up to the women's security line, I prepared my final thoughts as a severe woman in a black chador inspected her ticket, her back to two large portraits of the ayatollahs. "I just hope that after you finish, you'll come back," I whispered. "It's not really important how much you earn. Your lifestyle isn't expensive, and we can help you. I just want you to be certain of one thing. I know it's not always easy here," I said, casting a glance at the dour women in the chador and the portraits of the clerics on the wall, "but know that your heart will be more comfortable in a country that is your own." A lump rose in my throat. I arranged my features in what Negar calls my "serious face," pressed her through the security curtain, and fled.

The first week her absence hung the heaviest. I'm not usually given to nostalgia, especially the cloying sort common to Iranian mothers who perpetually live in their children's past. But that week the most ordinary smell or sound drew me back to Negar's adolescence. To the summer when she was studying for her college entrance exams and demanded absolute quiet, forcing her father and me into the bathroom to listen to the news on the radio. To the dark year when intellectuals were turning up dead all over the country and she crept into my study with a sly smile, waving the Agatha Christie novel *And Then There Were None.* To the night before her graduation, when she put her hands on her hips and said, "Don't tell me tomorrow that so-and-so is on hunger strike or that someone just got sent to prison. You *better* show up."

*F*ortunately, the year Negar left Iran my work kept me busier and more distracted than ever before. It was 2003, three years after the reformists swept the Majlis, or parliament, with a landslide victory and fourteen progressive female MPs entered the legislature. But for those three years, the women had no place to sit. Literally, they had no chairs. You would think if they could get themselves elected to parliament in the Islamic Republic, they might have been able to arrange for some chairs. Or at least complain publicly over the awkwardness of their seating in the legislature. They did neither, and I found out myself only by accident.

That year, one of the female MPs approached me to draft a resolution on family law. "Write something that broadens women's rights, but in a way that's compatible with Islam," she requested, "so that we can defend it on the floor." I agreed, and one afternoon the women's faction invited me to lunch at the parliament building, so we could discuss my draft. I drove downtown to the old building on Sepah Boulevard and parked not far from its stone facade. At lunch, I was pleased to find the food at the Majlis cafeteria neither too fancy nor self-consciously lumpen. Lunches in Iran had too long carried messages about status: under the shah's regime, lunchtime jaunts to restaurants in Paris reflected the height of sybaritism; in the early days of the revolution, lunches were excessively sloppy and canteen-like, to underscore the triumph of the Muslim proletariat. This lunch was just a normal lunch, which after decades of meals freighted with meaning was a very good thing.

After tea, we retired to the women's private chamber to talk. As we neared the end of the hallway, the first alarming sign was that their chamber didn't actually have a door, just a curtain. We entered an empty room whose floor was covered with a machine-woven rug. I kept looking for another door, the one that would lead into the room where they actually sat and worked. But they all put down their things and sat down cross-legged on the rug. "Why are there no chairs?" I asked. "Why is there not even a copy machine in here? This is the *parliament!*" "Well, we've asked for a copy machine lots of times," one of the MPs told me, "but they told us we were too few to justify having our own office equipment. We're allowed to use the men's offices, of course, but we prefer to be here, because it's usually so hot, and at least here we can take off our chadors and breathe a little."

Right then and there my heart broke a little. Here we were in parliament, inside the very halls where these women were supposed to legislate and change the conditions outside for millions and millions of women, and they couldn't even secure themselves a table. What can you accomplish in society at large when this is all you have achieved inside the institution itself? It was so hot, and the folds of our *roopooshes* and chadors so heavy, that we peeled them off and reclined on the rug. One of the MPs stretched out and began to nap.

"I think you'll quite like my solution," I began. I explained the draft of the law, how it included everything we sought in terms of divorce rights, embedded in sharia in a way that was wholly defendable. The MPs loved it. "Wonderful," one of them said, "but please stay quiet for now about the fact that you're this bill's author. Not everyone in this parliament is a reformist. There are fundamentalists too, influential ones, and if they find out you wrote the bill it might be doomed."

Two months later, the bill was clogged in the various Majlis commissions for preapproval, before it could even go to a vote. The MPs hadn't been able to convince the commissions that the bill was in concordance with Islamic law, and they asked me to come in and defend its compliance. I agreed, and arrived at the parliament building the next afternoon. About twenty MPs were present, most of them turbaned clerics; there were just two women.

The most important section of the bill pertained to divorce. In the reading of Islam from which the present law was derived, a man could divorce a woman with ease; basically, he could shout, "I divorce you! I divorce you! I divorce you!" under a tree or at the local kabob house and the deed was done. For a woman, securing a divorce was nearly impossible; she had to request her husband's written per-

mission to even initiate the process and was obliged to prove his in-
sanity, infertility, or other grave unfitness to see it through.

Classical Islamic law, or sharia, did not always treat divorce so in-
flexibly, but the drafters of the Iranian code had opted for the most
rigid interpretation. One school of thought in sharia, for example,
holds that if a woman forfeits her *mehrieh* (marriage allowance) she
can divorce her husband on the simple grounds of disliking him.
The intent of that approach is to allow a woman unilateral exit from
a marriage, with the price of forfeiting the *mehrieh* that would be her
due in the case of unfitness or consensual divorce. But the Iranian
law dealing with divorce on grounds of dislike demanded a relin-
quishment of the marriage allowance *and* the man's consent, making
it both difficult for a woman to secure and financially disadvanta-
geous at the same time.

I had spent hours with old legal tomes, drafting my law. Islamic
law had been handed down and studied centuries ago, and its
practitioners—seminarians, jurists, and lawyers alike—consulted
ancient texts as sources. Over the centuries, Islamic legal scholars
had anticipated nearly all circumstances that men and women
would encounter being on this earth together and had neatly
outlined the sharia position on each. They had imagined that in
some cases a woman would want to divorce her husband not
because he was infertile, mentally ill, or abusive but simply because
she did not like him, and they'd provided a way for her to extricate
herself. In drafting the law, I had anchored each proposed
provision in the old texts.

As I was defending the bill to the commission, an imperious, traditionalist cleric sitting next to me gathered his robes and turned to
address me: "Why have you written that male consent is not required
for divorce?"

"Because it's not," I said. "And I'll prove it to you." I pulled out
the *Sharh-e Lomeh,* the Shia Textbook of Jurisprudence. "This is the
book you study in the seminary, and on which you are tested in be-

coming a mullah," I stated. "It says nowhere in here that male consent is required. So why are you insisting that it is?"

He didn't say a word, but I noticed him summoning a clerk.

A moment later, another clerk tapped me on the shoulder. "There's a phone call for you," he said. I was surprised. I didn't think I had told anyone that I would be in parliament that afternoon. Surmising that perhaps it was a family emergency, I hurried out.

"Where's the phone?" I asked him out in the hallway.

"Oh, there's no phone call. We have heard enough from you, and they want to move to a vote. And no one else can be inside when they're voting."

"Can I at least go back and get my purse and my papers?"

"No, stay here. I'll go get them for you."

Before he scurried off, I remembered that a female representative from the judiciary was still inside the chambers. "Why can she stay during a vote and not me?" I asked.

The clerk hemmed. "Well, she's from the judiciary. She's different."

I started to wonder, Is it possible that they're not about to vote at all but have just thrown me out? Are they so shameless as to physically remove me from a debate?

That night one of the MPs called me at home. "I'm *so* sorry," she said. "We didn't even realize for half an hour that they'd thrown you out. When we realized what had happened we protested. But at any rate, please accept our apologies."

In the end, the bill didn't pass. I didn't understand why the female bloc hadn't proposed it earlier in their term, so that they would have had a good two years to fight. Perhaps the lack of a table or a copy machine interfered with their ability to legislate. Who knows? That afternoon at the Majlis embodied how the hard-liners running Iran abandoned reason in their dealings with me. Sometimes they would throw up small obstacles, such as ejecting me from a session of parliament. Other times, they threatened me directly, hoping I would be frustrated by my own fear.

I remember one occasion in particular when I was warned to drop a case because it happened to concern the husband of a very close friend—Siamak Pourzand, a journalist who was married to Mehrangiz Kar, a fellow activist lawyer and my confidante of many years. In late 2001, the seventy-one-year-old Pourzand was arrested on vague charges that later amounted to "having links with monarchists and counterrevolutionaries," "spying and undermining state security," and "creating disillusionment among young people." At the time, the system's tolerance for the independent press was waning by the day, and at Friday prayers a prominent ayatollah had warned that an agent of the U.S. government had arrived in Iran with a suitcase full of cash to distribute to reformist journalists. The rhetoric signaled a fresh attempt to discredit independent-minded journalists, and Pourzand—whose daughter abroad openly backed the monarchist opposition—provided a natural first target.

While the system detained him, state television broadcast an interview in which a thinner and unnatural-sounding Pourzand "confessed" to collaborating with the Iranian opposition in exile. Several journalists and activists were then summoned to a security headquarters and harassed based on claims that Pourzand had allegedly made against them. I myself received a summons and was told I was among the people Pourzand had incriminated. The interrogator asked me whom I met when traveling abroad and the sort of predictable questions meant to trap one into disclosing politically questionable acquaintances.

A few nights earlier, when I had been returning home with my daughters around midnight, two strange men had accosted us on our block. They'd been loitering suspiciously, with a few wilted flower stems in their hands. They wanted legal consultation, they'd said, and they had not backed off when I'd told them they should call my office during working hours. At just that moment, guests from a wedding party up the block had streamed out to their cars, and the men had scrambled away, tossing the flower stems at me. I'd taken their startled behavior and sudden disappearance as a thwarted attempt on my life, and had said as much to a friend on the phone that night. Clearly my phone was tapped, because the interrogator now invoked that evening, and suggested I was spreading false fears of assassination to blemish the country's reputation. My interrogator added that they were fed up with me and said that if I continued my work, I would face spying charges, that my name would be connected to Pourzand's file. "This time you will be up against the wall, and it will be done legally," he warned ominously. He meant that I would face a firing squad.

Some months later, with international human rights organizations raining criticism on the government, Pourzand received a two-month furlough from prison. When he returned to confinement, he phoned me and asked why I never visited him in prison. "The law prevents me from visiting you unless you are my client," I explained. Meanwhile, his wife had appealed to a parliamentary commission to pursue his case. When it became clear that there was no progress on this front, I followed up and was informed that pursuing his case would do more harm than good. Pourzand remained in detention, his health failing.

Thus I confronted yet another approach meant to intimidate me into surrendering my legal work. The episode reflected on just how many fronts the system sought to make people like myself, journalists and activists alike, vulnerable. We were entangled and implicated in the trumped-up legal cases of others, then stymied in the arenas where we sought to take our own work forward.

When I'd trumped that cleric in parliament with his own seminary's textbook, when there'd been nothing humanly possible left for him to argue, he had not surrendered but had resorted to force. The encounter also reflected the challenge of negotiating women's rights in the theocratic Iran of today. My draft law, which relied not on some fringe school of Islamic thought but on the central texts taught in the holy city of Qom's seminaries, showed that a basic right for women could be guaranteed within an Islamic framework of governance, provided those in government were inclined to interpret the faith in the spirit of equality.

In Islam, there exists a tradition of intellectual interpretation and innovation known as *ijtihad*, practiced by jurists and clerics over the centuries to debate the meaning of Koranic teachings as well as their application to modern ideas and situations. Sunni Islam effectively closed the door to *ijtihad* several centuries back, but in Shia Islam, the process and spirit of *ijtihad* thrive. *Ijtihad* is central to Islamic law, because sharia is more a set of principles than a codified set of rules. A decision or opinion derived from the process of *ijtihad* means that a jurist appraises a given matter (for example, should women be stoned for adultery in the twentieth century?) by applying reason and deduction and weighing the priorities of the concerns involved. In the early years after the revolution, Ayatollah Khomeini ruled that state media could broadcast music despite the severe attitude of the senior clergy toward song. He concluded that otherwise young people would be lured by Western radio and that ultimately this would be more wounding to the Islamic Republic. This was an act of *ijtihad*, in which a seventh-century convention was found unsuitable for the day.

On the one hand, *ijtihad* imposes flexibility on Islamic law and creates an exciting space for adapting Islamic values and traditions to our lives in the modern world. But this flexibility is also precisely what makes *ijtihad*, and Islamic jurisprudence altogether, a tricky foundation on which to base inalienable, universal rights. *Ijtihad* frees us by removing the burden of definitiveness—we can interpret and reinterpret Koranic teachings forever; but it also means clerics can take the Universal Declaration of Human Rights home and argue about it richly for centuries. It means it is possible for everyone, always, to have a point. It means that patriarchal men and powerful authoritarian regimes who repress in the name of Islam can exploit *ijtihad* to interpret Islam in the regressive, unforgiving manner that suits their sensibilities and political agendas. As with the mullah who summoned his clerk and removed me from the floor of parliament, fighting for women's rights in the Islamic Republic is often not a battle of wits or reason, nor is it always a fair fight. This does not mean that Islam and equal rights for women are incompatible; it means that invoking Islam in a theocracy refracts the religion through a kaleidoscope, with interpretations perpetually shifting and mingling and the vantage of the most powerful prevailing.

The experience of the Iranian reform movement—the Khatami tenure and the brief term of a pro-reform parliament—demonstrated the limitation of Islamic reform under the theocratic regime. In the late nineties, and even into the millennium, debates about Islamic reform dominated Iranian political circles. Progressive clerics and popular lay intellectuals and philosophers outlined their vision of an Islamic reformation and the path by which the Islamic Republic could be democratized from within. But the reform movement's failure called into question the relevance of the whole debate. What use was a reformist, tolerant brand of Islam if the theocratic constitution of the Islamic Republic and its powerful old-guard defenders considered their interpretation divinely sanctioned and nonnegotiable?

The brave journalist Akbar Ganji, in recent times the country's most important political prisoner, came up with a solution while serving time in prison for criticizing the regime. I have mentioned Ganji before, for it was his newspaper articles that linked the dissident murders of the late nineties to senior regime officials. If the taboos were falling left and right in the Islamic Republic, it was because people like him had sacrificed their lives—their health, their careers, and their families—along the way. In 2000, Ganji was sentenced to a six-year jail term for his articles. While serving time in Evin, Ganji wrote a book called *A Manifesto for Republicanism,* in which he advocated a full separation between religion and the state and called on the supreme leader to step down. His manifesto, as he'd surely intended, set off a great noise in the Islamic Republic. It was the first time a prominent dissident, a believing Muslim and former revolutionary at that, had called for the Islamic system to be replaced by a secular democracy. Ganji wrote that most Iranians did not lack an awareness of democracy; they were just reluctant to pay its price. He counseled civil disobedience and, at the very least, a strategy of "noncooperation with the despot."

I would run into him occasionally at Evin Prison, when I stopped there to visit my clients. One afternoon, when he said hello, I asked him, "Why is there not a peep about you and your work in the press? People are slowly forgetting about you." I couldn't understand; in cases like Ganji's, nearly all the work of a defense lawyer was advocacy and press work.

"I chose a bad lawyer," he said. "The authorities indicated that if I chose him to represent me, the court would reduce my sentence. But as you can see, it hasn't turned out that way. In three years, he hasn't visited me once in prison. Once I saw him in the prison yard, and he turned his face and pretended not to see me. What can I do? I'm stuck here."

I offered on the spot to take on his case, and a joyful look broke out on his impish face. But by the time I picked up his file, there was not much that could be done for him. The authorities barred me from seeing him, despite the fact that I was his lawyer and therefore the law guaranteed us visitation rights. The sentence was final, and the judiciary had no inclination to budge on the case of someone who had unleashed a scandal of historic magnitude before prison, and had then called for an end to the Islamic system from his cell. In the last year of his sentence, perhaps because he suspected that it would be extended, he launched a hunger strike, demanding his unconditional release from prison. It was a game of chicken, ultimately, with the hard-line clerics, to see who would blink first. Days passed and Ganji lost kilo after kilo until, fifty days into his hunger strike, doctors warned that he would sustain irreparable brain damage, and he relented.

In the end, I mention Akbar Ganji because his fight illustrates one of the ways change is taking place in Iran. By the time of his hunger strike, the press no longer operated in the atmosphere of relative freedom and independence enjoyed in the early reform era of 1999. Many Iranians, I found, had not heard the news of Ganji's hunger strike, but his manifesto did circulate. The difference between today and the Iran of 1979 is that information technology and the Internet have made blackout censorship impossible. When I saw televised photos of Ganji's emaciated body in the hospital, I thought only that generations to come would appreciate his sacrifice.

On a balmy evening in June 2003, over a thousand students gathered at an east Tehran university and lit rows of candles in vigil for fellow students injured after protests earlier that day. "Khatami, your silence defends this killing," they chanted, marching about the campus, calling for the president's resignation.

Five days earlier, students at another Tehran university had held a demonstration ostensibly against increases in university tuition, the pretext under which students had held anti-government protests in my own college days. Students at other universities heard of the rally and organized their own. Swiftly, the scattered protests gathered momentum and devolved into a sustained wave of unrest that drew large crowds calling for the end of the Islamic system. In previous years, student protests of this sort had taken the form of mild-mannered sit-ins, with slogans calling for freedom of speech, the release of political prisoners, and changes in the law. This time, students showed up armed with backpacks full of rocks and screamed for the system to be changed. The youthful hope that underpinned the reform movement had given way to despair and raw anger.

On the sixth evening of the unrest, which had wrought mayhem throughout Tehran, the authorities deployed their security forces around the city, determined to regain control of the streets. Under the silver light of a nearly full moon, Islamic vigilantes in beards and untucked shirts set up checkpoints around the squares, plainclothes security forces patrolled corners, and police cars blocked off roads leading to the universities. If you had chanced to drive through the city after midnight, you would have thought Tehran was at war. Long columns of soldier-laden trucks and police vehicles moved down the expressways, as though to battle.

The system crushed the protests with typical brutality, exacerbated this time by what it deemed American support for a challenge to its authority. "This is the beginning of people expressing themselves toward a free Iran, which I think is positive," President Bush had told reporters. Public American support for any pro-democracy phenomenon in Iran, whether from an individual or a trend or a demonstration, always provoked the Islamic system's ire and generally resulted in an even harsher crackdown. This time was no different.

State television broadcast footage of detained protesters, who sat bruised and sullen before the camera, recanting their participation. Student associations began releasing names of the estimated four thousand students who had gone missing since the start of the protests. Friends and family of missing detainees trekked up to the one place in Tehran you go when someone disappears during a protest: Evin Prison. After major disturbances, parents usually line the curb outside the prison, searching for news of their children. The scene is poignant and visually arresting, mothers wrapped in their black chadors, sitting disconsolately on the cement curb, against the backdrop of the mountainside prison.

Because photojournalists cannot tell a story without images, an Iranian-Canadian photographer named Zahra Kazemi drove up to the prison on June 23 to take pictures. The up-to-date government-issued press card in her bag, she thought, made it permissible for her to work around the city. When a prison guard spotted her taking photos, instead of asking her to stop, he demanded that she turn over her camera. Worried that officials might harass the families whose photos she had already taken, she flashed her press card and exposed the film to the light. The guard angrily yelled at her, "I didn't ask you to expose your film, I told you to give me your camera." "You can have the camera," she retorted, "but the film belongs to me." She was detained, and was interrogated over the next three days by police officers, prosecutors, and intelligence officials.

One of those afternoons, a friend of mine came by my office and said that a friend of hers by the name of Ziba, which is what Zahra Kazemi's friends called her, had been arrested. "Her family doesn't know," she said, "and I'm afraid to contact the Canadian embassy, because they called her a spy when they arrested her. What if they trace me contacting the embassy and accuse me of spying too?" "Just call the embassy from a pay phone, and don't introduce yourself," I said. "They need to know."

Four days later, Ziba was admitted to a Tehran hospital. Newspapers began running stories of an Iranian-Canadian photographer's arrest, calling her a spy who had entered the country undercover as a journalist. Only a week later did her relatives learn that she was no longer in custody but in a coma, in an intensive care unit guarded by security agents. A week after that, she died.

From the moment her death was made public, the case turned into an ugly, contested dispute involving the hard-line judiciary, the government of President Khatami, and the government of Canada. Ziba held Canadian as well as Iranian citizenship, and Canada swiftly pressed the Iranian government to return her body to Montreal and to punish her killers. The system claimed that she had suffered a stroke while under interrogation, though this unconvincing account was later changed to a story about how the photojournalist had fallen and hit her head. Only when one of Iran's vice presidents, Mohammad Ali Abtahi, came forward to admit that she had died as a result of being beaten did the hard-line system realize how difficult her death would be to cover up. In fact, it seemed taken off guard by the crescendo of condemnation that echoed around the world.

Not long after the newspapers announced Ziba's death and the system began contradicting itself as to its cause, another friend of hers called me and asked if she could visit me, along with Ziba's mother. They arrived at my office late one afternoon, and we drank tea together slowly as they recounted their stories.

Ziba's friend said that security officials had twice showed up at her house, where Ziba had been staying at the time of her arrest. "They kept asking me about her 'medical condition,' and what medicines she took daily," she said. "When I told them she's never been sick, they asked to see her things. I took them into the bathroom, and they began sorting through her toiletries. They seized on a bottle of multivitamins and a small packet of calcium supplements. 'See!' they said triumphantly, waving the bottles in the air. 'We told you she's sick.' 'Those are vitamins,' I said. 'You needn't be sick to take them.' I only realized later that they wanted to claim that Ziba had a preexisting condition that had simply worsened in prison."

Ziba's mother, a fragile, elderly woman with no other children besides her one daughter, had traveled all the way from Shiraz, a fabled city in southern Iran, to see me. When she began to speak, her voice trembled, and she paused every few moments, as though out of breath. "They called me in Shiraz," she said, "and told me, 'Zahra has been arrested and is in prison; come see her if you wish.' I boarded a bus to Tehran that very night, so I could arrive in the prison by morning. When I went to the prison administration office, they kept me waiting for two or three hours, and occasionally someone would appear and ask, 'What medicine did Ziba take?' 'I'm here to see my daughter,' I told them. 'Stop interrogating me. She was in perfect health. What has happened, that you're asking me such questions?'

"Until four that afternoon," she went on, "no one would answer me. Finally, as they were preparing to leave for the day, an administrator told me that Ziba was sick and had been taken to the hospital. I could go visit her there, he said. So I found a taxi and went to the hospital. When I entered her room, I couldn't believe it was my daughter, lying motionless on the bed, her face covered with an oxygen mask, strapped to all these blinking machines. I approached her bedside and gently lifted the hospital gown, to see what had happened to her. Her breasts, her arms, the insides of her thighs were all scratched up, and mottled with angry, blue-gray bruises.

"The next day, I went back to see her again. This time, they wouldn't let me inside the room but permitted me to peer in through its window. She seemed to be in precisely the same position I had left her yesterday, and then I knew that she was only being kept alive by machines. I knew I had lost my only child.

"While she was still in a coma, my grandson in Canada urged me to send her body back there for burial. When I told the authorities from the judiciary and the Ministry of Intelligence that this was the family's decision, they insisted the body be buried in Iran. They threatened me. They said they would forever harass all of Ziba's friends here if we did not agree. I was upset and confused, worried about what might happen if I said no. So I consented, and scarcely hours after she finally died, a plane flew her body to Shiraz for burial."

When Ziba's mother paused to take a sip of tea, I imagined her confronting such intimidation alone, and my heart felt heavy. Neither literate nor easily mobile, she had consented when a smooth-talking, court-appointed lawyer from Tehran had knocked on her door in Shiraz and asked her to sign over power of attorney, so he could track down Ziba's killers. She'd signed the papers without reading them, and realized only later that night, when she showed a copy to a relative, that she had signed over the right not just to litigate the case but to settle as well. Her relatives advised her to find a proper lawyer, and that is how she had made her way to me.

"I can't afford to pay you," she said haltingly. "That's fine," I quickly reassured her. "I wouldn't accept money from you anyway. But let's get down to business." I immediately wrote a letter on her behalf, addressed to the court, nullifying her agreement with the court-appointed lawyer. And then we began to prepare for the trial, which was to start the following week.

On the first day of the trial I stayed home, and I instructed Ziba's mother to do the same. I didn't want the court to know that I was representing her, for under Iranian law, the court decides on the trial's first day whether to hold open or closed proceedings. I knew that if I showed up it would immediately be designated a closed trial. Ziba's mother sent a letter from Shiraz that said, "My lawyer is God." During the opening session, the head of the court figured that if there was no lawyer and if Ziba's mother hadn't even bothered to travel from Shiraz, it would be a token gesture of goodwill to declare the trial open. My little ruse worked, as the court could not reverse its decision.

Ten days later I was scheduled to leave for a trip to Paris—the same trip during which I learned I had won the Nobel Prize—but I made sure to see Ziba's mother before leaving. Ziba was not the first person to die in an Iranian prison, but it was the first time a death in custody had attracted such international attention. By representing her family, I wanted to show the world what transpired in Iran's prisons, and hopefully prevent such careless brutality from repeating itself. The court proceedings fell short of our expectations, and the judge later said it was impossible to identify the official who had struck the fatal blow to Ziba. But that day, her mother and I focused on our legal strategy. She had brought me Shirazi lemons, and their scent wafted throughout the office, the same way the orange blossoms of Shiraz perfume the air in the spring.

CHAPTER TWELVE

The Nobel Prize

In September 2003, I was invited to attend a seminar in Paris on the city of Tehran. The Iranian embassy in France initially protested my participation, on the grounds that I held beliefs counter to the official position of the Iranian government. Even abroad, it seemed, the system believed it could control what was said or thought about Iran, and considered views contradicting its own illegitimate. The embassy threatened to prevent Iranian films and works of art destined for the seminar from leaving the country if I participated. The municipality of Paris, the seminar's organizer, stuck fast to its position, and the Iranian government eventually relented.

I brought my younger daughter, Nargess, along, and in between seminar screenings of films such as *SOS Tehran*, I gave her a tour of Paris, taking quiet pleasure in her delight at the Eiffel Tower and the Louvre, the Champs-Élysées and the grand architecture. We stayed in a hotel until the last night of our trip, when we were invited to the home of an old friend of mine from the prerevolutionary judiciary, Dr. Abdol-Karim Lahiji, now the vice president of the International Federation of Human Rights Leagues. Our visit came too quickly to an end, and the next morning we packed our bags so his wife could drop us off at the airport. In all honesty, I had heard sometime back that my name had at one point been on the list of candidates for the Nobel Peace Prize, but an Iranian newspaper had reported that it had been deleted, so I didn't give the matter much thought at all, and never switched on the television or the radio while in Paris.

That morning, Dr. Lahiji said good-bye to us before going to work, and as we hauled our suitcases to the door, the phone rang. It was for me, so I walked back into the kitchen and picked up the receiver. On the other end of the line, a man introduced himself as calling from the Nobel Peace Prize committee. He asked me to stay near the phone for some important news. Assuming that one of my friends was playing a prank, I put down the receiver impatiently. Ten minutes later, another call came, with the same message. I explained that I was en route to the airport and had to go, but the caller insisted that the news was urgent. When he realized I didn't believe him and was close to hanging up again, he passed the phone to another voice, who explained that I was a candidate for the prize and should just wait a few minutes longer. I overheard somebody say that I had won the Nobel Peace Prize and sat there dumbfounded, wondering whether I should catch my flight back to Tehran or not.

The phone started ringing incessantly, with calls from journalists. I called Dr. Lahiji at work and asked him if had heard any such news. I was in shock, really, and wasn't sure what to do next. He suggested that I postpone my flight, because it was hard to predict how the Iranian government would react. In Tehran, he reasoned, reporters and journalists from around the world wouldn't really have access to me, so it was better to stay put for now. In two hours, he said, he would arrange a press conference for me.

I arrived to a crowded room filled with reporters, who began firing questions at me before I even took the podium. The questions

At the Paris press conference after winning the Nobel Prize.

whizzed back and forth, and I answered as swiftly and articulately as I could manage. After the announcement of the prize, an emissary from the Iranian embassy in Paris approached me, and in a stiff and formal manner informed me that the ambassador sent his congratulations. They assumed that immediately upon receipt of the prize, I would begin raining invective on the Islamic Republic. That was not, and indeed never had been, my intention. When they sat through the press conference and realized that my pronouncements were the same as ever, measured and civil, they sent two people over from the embassy with a Koran, as a present. They said the ambassador had wanted to see me, but that he had a previous engagement and was willing to speak to me on the phone. They put a call through on a cell phone, and we spoke briefly.

Once the press conference concluded, I paused for a second and realized that I needed to phone my mother, to explain that I wouldn't be arriving in Tehran on my scheduled flight but would take the same one the next day. My brother phoned later that evening from Tehran and told me that a welcoming committee had been formed to greet me upon my arrival. Apparently there was confusion about what part of the airport to use, and I insisted on not being taken through the government's VIP reception area. The welcome committee also disagreed, it seemed, on when I should return. Some said it would be better for me to wait for a proper setup at the airport, to give people time to arrive in Tehran from the provinces; others said we needed to ride the spontaneity of the moment and get me back to Tehran in time to celebrate with Iranians while the news was fresh. For my part, the incessant interviews and whirlwind was wearying, and despite the confusion, I wanted to go home.

The next day at the airport, well-wishers flocked to see me off before my flight. Dr. Lahiji and I said our good-byes in a meeting room the embassy had reserved. On board the plane, the Iran Air flight captain came over to congratulate me and moved Nargess and me up to the first-class cabin. Soon the stewardess started ferrying notes of congratulations from the other passengers. They kept coming, until I decided to walk through the plane and shake hands with people. The passengers were bubbling over with excited congratulations, save two very serious men, who warned that I should be careful not to undermine the honor of those who had shed their blood for the people and Islam. "The honor of the martyrs," I said, "is so valuable that it cannot be blemished by a single individual; but please rest assured."

The captain announced that he was calling our journey the Flight of Peace, and he invited my daughter and me up to the cockpit. When we got there, he turned away from the flashing lights of the console to speak with us, and for a second I feared the plane might crash. "Can I ask why you're not looking ahead?" I said nervously. He explained that the plane was on autopilot, and I felt quite silly.

Only after we returned to our seats did I have a quiet moment to lean my head against the seatback and reflect on what it all meant. My thoughts came quick and fast: Our struggling NGO could finally have office furniture... What would the Iranian government think?... Would I be safer, somehow protected by this prize in the name of peace?... Or would it aggravate those in Iran whose tolerance for me was already limited, who had planned to have me killed when I was infinitely less prominent?

As the sky we flew through darkened and the bustle of the cabin settled, I began to consider the prize's real meaning. Not for a second had I thought it was meant for me as an individual. Such lofty recognition could only be intended for what someone's life symbolized, the path or approach they had followed in pursuit of some higher purpose. In the last twenty-three years, from the day I was stripped of my judgeship to the years doing battle in the revolutionary courts of Tehran, I had repeated one refrain: an interpretation of Islam that is in harmony with equality and democracy is an authentic expression of faith. It is not religion that binds women, but the selective dictates of those who wish them cloistered. That belief, along with the conviction that change in Iran must come peacefully and from within, has underpinned my work.

I have been under attack most of my adult life for this approach, threatened by those in Iran who denounce me as an apostate for daring to suggest that Islam can look forward and denounced outside my country by secular critics of the Islamic Republic, whose attitudes are no less dogmatic. Over the years, I have endured all manner of slights and attacks, been told that I must not appreciate or grasp the real spirit of democracy if I can claim in the same breath that freedom and human rights are not perforce in conflict with Islam. When I heard the statement of the prize read aloud, heard my religion mentioned specifically alongside my work defending Iranians' rights, I knew at that moment what was being recognized: the belief in a positive interpretation of Islam, and the power of that belief to aid Iranians who aspire to peacefully transform their country.

As the twinkling lights of Tehran grew visible beneath us and the plane began its descent, my daughter reached over to pat my shoulder. The plane skidded to a stop on the tarmac, and the flight attendant asked me to disembark first, guiding me to the door of the plane. When it swung open, the first thing I saw was my mother's shining face. I took her soft, wrinkled hands in mine and pressed them against my lips. And then I leaned back and finally noticed the crowd, stretching out as far as I could see. Ayatollah Khomeini's granddaughter stepped forward and placed a wreath of delicate orchids around my neck. The crowd surged forward on all sides, and I flung a protective arm around my mother's thin shoulders, looking to the security officers around us, who seemed at a loss for what to do. I cannot win the Nobel Prize and then be crushed by a welcome crowd, I thought wryly, and decided to give the police an opportunity to form a ring around us. I inhaled a great breath and belted out the loudest *Allaho akbar!* I could manage. Everyone, from the airport crew to the thousands of citizens, froze in surprise, and in that second the police surrounded us and guided us away to a waiting room.

Both a popular vice president and a government spokesman—members of the then reformist branch of the system—awaited us there and greeted me warmly. We exchanged a few words, then quickly moved toward a makeshift scaffolding that had been constructed for my arrival, since it was pushing midnight and from the dull roar outside I could tell the crowd must number in the hundreds of thousands. I could not believe my eyes when they finally hoisted me up. People extended out in all directions, filling the whole terminal area of the airport and reaching far beyond, down the long boulevard that leads into the city. The last time such a great human mass had descended on Tehran airport, the year was 1979 and the figure on board the flight from Paris was Ayatollah Khomeini. Only this time, you could see from the mass of head scarves that women composed the majority of the crowd. Some wore the black chador, but most bright veils, and the gladioluses and white roses they waved in the air flashed in the dark of the night. "They walked here," my brother whispered

At the Tehran airport after winning the Nobel Prize.

Most of the people who greeted me at the airport were women.

in my ear. "They drove until the roads were jammed, left their cars, and walked. The flights have all been canceled because all the roads to the airport are blocked with people."

In the distance, a group of university students stood together, singing "Yar-e Dabestani," a bittersweet folk song that has become the anthem of young pro-democracy organizers. Usually they sing it at sit-ins, to keep their spirits up before the paramilitaries rush to attack them, and on all those occasions where they come together, fearful about the future but determined enough to assemble together, in and of itself a risk. The melody is sorrowful but galvanizing, and for the first time in longer than I cared to remember I felt hopeful when they reached the line "Whose hands but mine and yours can pull back these curtains?"

There was no proper microphone system set up for me to address such a vast crowd, so I apologized and waved, and eventually climbed back down. As we finally made our way to the car and slowly drove

Maxppp/Reflex News

Receiving the Nobel Prize.

forward, the crowds parted to let us ahead, and through the window I watched the faces slide by, hopeful, serious, proud, but, most of all, so *alive*. Near the arched monument built by the shah in south Tehran now renamed Freedom Square, I caught sight of a woman with a child in one hand, a makeshift poster in the other, and the sight made my breath catch, for her sign read, "This is Iran."

Epilogue

PROPPED UP ON MY DESK IN TEHRAN IS A CLIPPING OF a political cartoon I like to keep in sight while I work. The sketch is of a woman wearing a space-age battle helmet, bent over a blank page with a pen in her hand. It reminds me of a truth that I have learned in my lifetime, one that is echoed in the history of Iranian women across the ages: that the written word is the most powerful tool we have to protect ourselves, both from the tyrants of the day and from our own traditions. Whether it is the storyteller of legend Scheherazade, staving off beheading by spinning a thousand and one tales, feminist poets of the last century who challenged the culture's perception of women through verse, or lawyers like me, who defend the powerless in courts, Iranian women have for centuries relied on words to transform reality.

Though words are peaceful weapons, over the past fifteen years I have been harassed, threatened, and jailed in the course of defending human rights and victims of violence in Iran. I have long wanted to write a memoir of these years, told from the perspective of a woman who was sidelined by the Islamic Revolution but stayed in Iran and carved out a professional and political role

in the forbidding theocracy that emerged. Along with my own journey, I wanted to illustrate how Iran was changing, for change comes to
the Islamic Republic in slow and subtle ways that are easy to miss.
Standing at a crowded intersection of the capital or listening to the
sermon at Friday prayers, you would not immediately know that 65
percent of Iran's university students and 43 percent of its salaried
workers are women. I wanted to write a book that would help correct
Western stereotypes of Islam, especially the image of Muslim women
as docile, forlorn creatures. The censorship that prevails in the Islamic
Republic has made it impossible to publish an honest account of my
life here. My work places me in opposition to our system, and I suspect I may never be able to write anything in Iran without taking off
the helmet.

When I received the Nobel Peace Prize in 2003, I believed that at
least in the West, in open societies that protected freedom of expression, I could publish a memoir that would help correct stereotypes
about Muslim women. I felt my experience could make a contribution to the accelerated debate about Islam and the West, and reach a
wide audience. Beyond helping shade the debate about Islamic civilization and its encounter with modern America, I felt that the cold
antagonism between the United States and Iran made communica-
tion between the two societies more urgent than ever. I imagined that
the voices of Iranians who do not feel their government and its
diplomats represent them would be especially welcome in America.

I shared my intention to write a book with a university professor
in the United States, my close friend Dr. Muhammad Sahimi, and
asked for his help. Dr. Sahimi, after speaking with a number of literary agents, introduced me to a woman named Wendy Strothman.
She had attended two of my talks at U.S. universities and felt strongly
that my story would find an eager audience among the American
people. The only obstacle, I was shocked to learn when we met in
May 2004, would be the American government. Sanctions regulations in the United States, it turned out, made it virtually impossible
for me to publish a memoir in America.

Despite federal laws that say U.S. trade embargoes may not restrict the free flow of information, the Treasury Department's Office of Foreign Assets Control (OFAC) regulated the import of books from Iran and other embargoed countries. Though the ban did not purport outright to obstruct the flow of information between nations, it effectively did so by prohibiting the publication of "materials not fully created and in existence." This meant that I could publish my memoir in the United States, but it would be illegal for an American literary agent, publisher, or editor to help me, and likely illegal for a publisher to advertise the work. Neither of us realized at first what serious penalties the regulations could carry. We soon learned that if Wendy had defied them, she could have been fined severely and possibly faced jail time.

In Iran, the Islamic system censors books, casts up Internet firewalls, and bans satellite television in an effort to prevent Iranians from accessing information from the outside world. It seemed incomprehensible to me that the U.S. government, the self-proclaimed protector of a free way of life, would seek to regulate what Americans could or could not read, a practice that is called censorship when enacted by authoritarian regimes. What was the difference between the censorship in Iran and this censorship in the United States?

American officials, when pressed by publishers about the regulations, linked them to national security and insisted that it was possible to petition for a special approval. But if defending victims in the courts of the Islamic Republic has taught me anything, it is that a single case is rarely the real battle; a case is a symptom of an injustice embedded in the law itself.

As a recipient of the Nobel Peace Prize, I stood a firm chance of receiving a special license, because I had been imprisoned in Iran for my defense of human rights and a ban on my memoir would have been difficult to defend. But such an exemption would do nothing for the hundreds of writers and scholars in Iran and other embargoed countries turned away by journals and publishers out of fear of the Treasury Department's regulations. The regulations were stymieing intellectual exchange in the humanities and the sciences, preventing scholars from sharing lessons learned from such tragedies as the 2003 earthquake in Bam, in which nearly thirty thousand Iranians died.

As a lifetime defender of free expression, I could not countenance the thought of applying for a government license to publish my book. I wished for no special treatment because of my unique celebrity, and for me the case swiftly turned into one of broader principles: the right to freedom of speech, and the right and responsibility of the American public to hear from voices around the world. Wendy agreed to do everything possible to help me fight the regulations, and we began seeking legal counsel to aid us in our effort. After a worrisome few months, we found Philip Lacovara, a distinguished lawyer who had argued the Watergate tapes case before the Supreme Court and a partner in the firm of Mayer, Brown, Rowe & Maw, which offered us pro bono counsel in taking on the U.S. government.

On October 26, 2004, Wendy and I filed a lawsuit against the Treasury Department in a federal court in New York, joining one filed in September by several American organizations representing publishers, editors, and translators. Our lawsuit challenged the standing regulations against import of "information materials" from embargoed countries and argued that they violated the rights of American readers under the First Amendment to the United States Constitution. In my declaration, I called the ban a critical missed opportunity, both for Americans to learn more about my country and its people from a variety of Iranian voices and for a better understanding to be achieved between our two nations.

To my mind, the regulations also reflected how tangled and dysfunctional the relationship between the United States and Iran remains to this day. The lack of honest exchange remains a dangerous habit for both countries. It has led both to sustain traumas singular in their modern history: the 1953 CIA overthrow of a democratic government in Iran and, its delayed response, the 1979 hostage siege of the U.S. embassy in Tehran. It worries me that despite this fraught record, the two countries persist in behaving as though their fates are not intertwined, as though they can muffle each other out and feel no ramifications.

For better or for worse, the United States is the sole superpower in the world today, and Iran is the most strategic country in a restive region vital to U.S. interests. The ensuing entanglements are not few: Iran's sphere of influence extends far into Iraq, where America uneasily presides over chaos, and the Iraqi government's new leaders are intimate friends of the Islamic Republic. And despite their government's official stance, Iranian young people remain cheerfully pro-American, the last pocket of such sentiment in an angry Middle East. The two nations know they share strategic interests; this recognition enabled them to join forces to sort out Afghanistan's future after the fall of the Taliban. But ideology and mutual suspicion play as much a role in their ongoing rift as realpolitik, which makes the exchange of ideas—essentially, access to each other's culture and attitudes beyond official rhetoric—so imperative.

On December 16, 2004, the Treasury Department revised its regulations on publications of works by citizens of embargoed nations. Had it not, it would have faced the prospect of a federal court striking down its policy as unconstitutional. Two months later, in his State of the Union speech, President Bush told the Iranian people, "As you stand for your own liberty, America stands with you." It is hard to imagine the president making this statement while Iranians' right to publish accounts of such stands in America was yet in peril.

In the long and violent history of our two countries, the Treasury Department's revision is a modest step, but its symbolic value is of great encouragement to me. Is it not remarkable, in the end, that an Iranian woman living in her home country could have led to the effort that made the U.S. government's practices more just? It was a victory I took back to Iran and spoke of frequently, for its instructiveness as we look forward. It allowed me to contradict what has become a political truism in the rhetoric of the Islamic Republic, that America understands only the language of force. Bellicosity and brinkmanship are what have brought us to where we stand now, but they remain ingrained habits for both sides. We may need a horizon of decades to wear down the present monolith of mistrust. But such small steps remind us that by using the political process to change each other's positions, our fates can be intertwined in ways that are fruitful.

I realize that putting so much store in political dialogue seems overly optimistic, given the gulf that exists between the West's expectations of Iran and the Iranian system's inclination to compromise. I focus on the political process not because I imagine we will refashion a new relationship around the negotiating table anytime soon but because I see no other options ahead. Iran, for its part, must peacefully transition to a democratic government that represents the will of the majority of Iranians. Between our still too recent revolution and the eight years that followed, Iranians are tired of bloodletting and violence. Many are ready to go to prison or risk their lives for their dissent, but I don't see Iran today as a country where people are ready to pick up weapons against their government.

The West, for its part, has the option of using diplomacy to pressure Iran to change its behavior, from its human rights record inside the country to the nature of its nuclear energy program. The threat of regime change by military force, while reserved as an option by some in the Western world, endangers nearly all of the efforts democracy-minded Iranians have made in these recent years. The threat of military force gives the system a pretext to crack down on its legitimate opposition and undermines the nascent civil society that is slowly taking shape here. It makes Iranians overlook their resentment of the regime and move behind their unpopular leaders out of defensive nationalism. I can think of no scenario more alarming, no internal shift more dangerous than that engendered by the West imagining that it can bring democracy to Iran through either military might or the fomentation of violent rebellion.

Most important, the West can keep Iran's human rights record in the spotlight, for the Islamic system has shown itself to be sensitive to such criticism. The Islamic Republic may hold firm to its right to nuclear power, even if it means suffering sanctions at the hands of the international community. But its more rational policy makers see a tainted human rights record as a self-inflicted wound that weakens Iran's bargaining power. If the clerics in power detect military strikes on the horizon instead of a negotiated solution, they will find no incentive, no credibility gained, in safeguarding the rights of their citizens. I see foreign pressure as useful, but it must be the right kind of pressure, targeted and with a purpose. For in the end, the Iranian Revolution has produced its own opposition, not least a nation of educated, conscious women who are agitating for their rights. They must be given the chance to fight their own fights, to transform their country uninterrupted.

The price of transforming Iran peacefully, I have long known but these days feel more acutely, is sacrifice of the highest order. It is simply a reality that people like myself or the dissidents I represent will be lost along the way. We know this only too well, for countless of our colleagues and acquaintances have been killed over these long years. The threats against my own life have stepped up since I received the Nobel Prize, and the Iranian government has appointed twenty-four-hour bodyguards for my protection. It goes without saying that this arrangement is, at best, an awkward one. There are times that feel more dangerous than others, moments when the political atmosphere in Tehran becomes so palpably tense that we speak in whispers, afraid almost of the air itself. At these moments, some of my friends and relatives suggest that I should spend some time abroad. What good am I abroad? I ask myself. The nature of my work, the role that I play in Iran, could it be conducted from across continents? Of course not. And so I remind myself that the greatest

threat of all is my own fear; that it is our fear, the fear of Iranians
✔ who want a different future, that makes our opponents powerful.

There are times, though, when I pause and contemplate slowing
down. I remember that I scarcely enjoyed my daughters' childhoods.
Of course I was there physically, packing those lunches and driving
them to school. But I was concentrating so fiercely on holding everything together—my own work, my anxieties, my health and theirs—
that I forgot to enjoy their sweetest years. Now that I have realized
this, they are grown up and gone, and so I contemplate slowing down
a little just for myself. I harbor no illusion of being able to retire, for
that would mean that Iran has changed, and that people like me are
no longer needed to protect Iranians from their government. If that
day comes in my lifetime, I will sit back and applaud the efforts of
the next generation from the seclusion of my garden. If it does not,
I will continue as I have done, in hopes that more of my fellow Iranians will stand at my side.

What I have recounted in this book is my personal recollection of
numerous cases and events, to the extent that they have affected my
life. It is not a political memoir, nor have I attempted to offer a political analysis of how and why certain events came to pass. Many of
the cases I describe deserve a much fuller treatment than they receive
here, and in the future I hope I can devote other books to exploring
them from a more analytical perspective.

Acknowledgments

I MUST FIRST THANK ABDOL-KARIM LAHIJI FOR YEARS OF indispensable guidance. I am deeply grateful to my trusted friend Muhammad Sahimi for all his advice and accumulated wisdom regarding my endeavors outside Iran. I am indebted to Mansour Farhang for friendship and counsel. The legal team of Philip Lacovara, Anthony Diana, and Ryan Farley of Mayer, Brown, Rowe & Maw made this book possible with their generous pro bono representation of our case against the U.S. Department of the Treasury. I thank my agent, Wendy Strothman, and her colleague Dan O'Connell of the Strothman Agency for their efforts in shepherding this book to publication in America. At Random House, David Ebershoff edited the manuscript with the gift of a storyteller and the acuity of a historian. His commitment to bringing this story to life for an American audience was a source of great inspiration. Finally, words cannot describe my deep appreciation for my co-author, Azadeh Moaveni, who combined her immense talent with countless hours and days of hard work to produce, from my original rough draft, the final version of this book.

Sources

Abrahamian, Ervand. *Tortured Confessions: Prisons and Public Recantations in Modern Iran.* Berkeley: University of California Press, 1999.

Behbahani, Farhad. Personal interview. 28 August 2005.

Boroujerdi, Mehrzad. *Iranian Intellectuals and the West: The Tormented Triumph of Nativism.* Syracuse: Syracuse University Press, 1996.

Forouhar, Parastou. Personal interview. 15 August 2005.

Human Rights Watch. "No Exit: Human Rights Abuses Inside the Mojahedin Khalq Camps." May 2005.

Kapuściński, Ryszard. *Shah of Shahs.* San Diego: Harcourt Brace Jovanovich, 1982.

Kar, Mehrangiz. "Prison's Revelations." *Payam-e Emrooz,* 2 February 2001.

Lahiji, Shahla. "Evin Hotel Is Further Down the Road." *Payam-e Emrooz,* 2 February 2001.

Milani, Abbas. *The Persian Sphinx: Amir Abbas Hoveyda and the Riddle of the Iranian Revolution.* Washington, D.C.: Mage Publishers, 2000.

Milani, Farzaneh. "Silencing a Modern Scheherazade." *Christian Science Monitor,* 17 November 2004.

Moghadam, Valentine. *Women, Work, and Ideology in Post-revolutionary Iran.* East Lansing: Michigan State University, 1988.

Mottahedeh, Roy. *The Mantle of the Prophet: Religion and Politics in Iran.* New York: Pantheon Books, 1985.

Rahnema, Ali. *An Islamic Utopian: A Political Biography of Ali Shariati.* London: I. B. Tauris, 2000.

Sahimi, Muhammad. Personal interview. 24 July 2005.

Sciolino, Elaine. *Persian Mirrors: The Elusive Face of Iran.* New York: Free Press, 2000.

Wilson, George. "Navy Missile Downs Iranian Jetliner." *Washington Post,* 4 July 1988, A1.

Wright, Robin. *The Last Great Revolution.* New York: Knopf, 2000.

Index

Page numbers in *italics* refer to illustrations.

ABOUT THE AUTHORS

SHIRIN EBADI, winner of the 2003 Nobel Peace Prize, is one of the world's leading human rights activists. She continues to work as a lawyer in Tehran, while also lecturing around the world. This is her first book for a Western audience.

AZADEH MOAVENI is the author of *Lipstick Jihad: A Memoir of Growing Up Iranian in America and American in Iran*. She has written for the *Los Angeles Times* and is *Time* magazine's Islamic affairs correspondent. She grew up in northern California and now lives in Tehran.

ABOUT THE TYPE

This book was set in Centaur, a typeface designed by the American typographer Bruce Rogers in 1929. Centaur was a typeface that Rogers adapted from the fifteenth-century type of Nicolas Jenson and modified in 1948 for a cutting by the Monotype Corporation.

Also available from Rider:

Making Terrorism History
Practical alternatives to the 'war on terror'

Scilla Elworthy and Gabrielle Rifkind

Resolving intractable conflicts has become an even more urgent task since the September 11 and 7 July attacks, and since the invasions of Afghanistan and Iraq. However, strategies which simply try to hit back at the 'enemy', the 'terrorists' or political opponents by using arms are counterproductive. They increase both the level of violence and the yawning chasm between the two sides.

This highly acclaimed book argues that we must address the emotional and psychological effects of violence and humiliation on whole communities, and the various economic, social and cultural issues that sustain cycles of terror. It outlines key approaches that can be used in Iraq, the Israel-Palestinian conflict, and also in our own towns and cities, to stop the spectre of rising terror and violence in our world.

Rabble-Rouser for Peace

The authorised biography of one of the world's best-loved peacemakers, Desmond Tutu

John Allen

Archibishop Desmond Tutu has become recognised as one of the world's most charismatic and inspirational spiritual leaders. Yet his experience during the Apartheid years in South Africa, and his chairing of the Truth and Reconciliation Commission, have made him much more than a church leader at home – more of a tireless worker for justice everywhere. This is the first book to tell the full story of how a boy from South Africa's poverty-stricken black townships became one of the world's best-known religious figures, a moral icon to those who work for peace, and a public figure with a place in history. On the one hand Tutu is a man of action who has literally kept the peace between warring factions on the streets of South Africa with nothing more than a megaphone – and on the other he is also a contemplative, thinking person able to tap into depths of spirituality and serenity for which so many people today are looking.

Buy Rider Books

Order further Rider titles from your local bookshop, or
have them delivered direct to your door by Bookpost

☐ Making Terrorism History   1846040477   £3.99
☐ Desmond Tutu: Rabble Rouser for Peace   1844135713   £18.99
☐ The Lucifer Effect   1844135772   £16.99
☐ Peace Is the Way   1844132978   £7.99

FREE POST AND PACKING
Overseas customers allow £2.00 per paperback

ORDER:

By phone: 01624 677237

By post: Random House Books
c/o Bookpost
PO Box 29
Douglas
Isle of Man, IM99 1BQ

By fax: 01624 670923

By email: bookshop@enterprise.net

Cheques (payable to Bookpost) and credit cards accepted

Prices and availability subject to change without notice.
Allow 28 days for delivery.
When placing your order, please mention if you do not wish to receive
any additional information

www.randomhouse.co.uk